JANET LOWE

THE MAN WHO BEATS THE S&P

INVESTING WITH
BILL MILLER

 JOHN WILEY & SONS, INC.

Published by John Wiley & Sons Canada, Ltd.

John Wiley & Sons Canada Limited
22 Worcester Road
Etobicoke, Ontario
M9W 1L1

National Library of Canada Cataloguing in Publication Data
Lowe, Janet
   The man who beats the S&P: investing with Bill Miller/Janet Lowe.

Includes index.
ISBN 0-470-83258-4

   1. Miller, Bill, 1950-. 2. Investments. I. Title.

HG4521.L832 2002   332.6   C2002-904184-8

Production Credits
Printer: Tri-Graphic Printing

Printed in Canada
10 9 8 7 6 5 4 3 2 1

This book is dedicated to the men, women, and children who lost their lives in the September 11, 2001, terrorist attack on the New York City World Trade Center and the United States Pentagon, and to all those who immediately went to work to rescue those whom they could, to help the loved ones of the victims, and to rebuild a better, stronger, braver America.

CONTENTS

Contents

Contents

Contents

INTRODUCTION

Bill Miller seems an unlikely candidate to be an investment superstar. Unlike George Soros, Miller doesn't make dramatic and risky plays that impact entire governments. Unlike Peter Lynch, he does not work for a major financial company that uses him as a marketing icon. Unlike Warren Buffett, he isn't a natural entertainer. Contemplative and soft-spoken, the tall, balding Miller is unstriking in his appearance. Except for his height and his refined manner, you might not even notice him in a crowd. Yet though he lacks the theatrical flair of some of his contemporaries, he has attracted a substantial following. And with good reason. By 2001, his record was indisputably the best in the mutual fund industry.

This book is about a man who has become an investment champion by looking for ideas everywhere—a quest that has led to surprisingly independent investment decisions. He reads old books, attends new age science seminars, and seeks out the best concepts he can find. Miller is a numbers guy who will tell you straight away that numbers alone won't do the job. Lisa Rapuano, a member of the Legg Mason mutual fund team, warned that there was no point in portraying Miller's techniques as simple or easy to follow. Simple they're not. However, they can be understood, and if an investor is willing to make the intellectual commitment, they can be followed.

Can you become a mirror image of Bill Miller by reading this book? Not likely. There are some individuals who consistently beat the market, but very few people can match their performance by imitation. "Their skill," Miller says, "isn't something that can be taught, since it's nonalgorithmic."[1] This is a typical Miller thing to say. He often sends people scurrying to their dictionaries.

1

While reading this book you should keep several things in mind. As head of Legg Mason's mutual fund unit, Miller manages or participates in the management of several funds. Most of the emphasis in this book, however, is on his flagship effort—the fund that made him famous, Legg Mason Value Trust–Primary. This is the fund that has set the performance records. Nevertheless, some of the stocks used for examples of investment decisions in this book were purchased solely for Special Investment Trust or Opportunity Trust. Some examples also come from Total Return Trust, which ceased to exist when it was merged into America's Leading Companies Fund. These funds are mentioned throughout the text to illustrate special points.

There is persistent speculation that Miller may branch out independently and establish his own company or may jump ship for a larger company than Legg Mason. Miller says that is unlikely. Why should he leave Legg Mason? What other employer would be as forbearing? "I can foul up here for a while before they lose patience," he jokes.[2]

Although this book is full of ideas, concepts, and principles, it is also heavy with numbers. To make reading easier, I've included charts and graphs that summarize the fundamental financial information on companies that have been important to the performance of Value Trust. The charts can be found in Appendix 4 at the back of the book. Because I often use terms or phrases that may be unfamiliar to the reader, there is a glossary and series of indices at the back of the book. Please refer to them liberally.

A number of people have made valuable contributions to this book. Austin Lynas has been of invaluable help in research and in creating the charts and graphs. Arthur Q. Johnson generously shared his wisdom and expertise. Alice Fried Martell, as always, has been the ideal literary agent. Joan O'Neil, Debra Englander, and all of the staff at John Wiley & Sons provided the highest-quality advice and help. Robert Hagstrom, Ernie Kiehne, Darlene Orange, Jennifer Murphy, Mark Niemann, Lisa Rapuano, Dale Wettlaufer, and others at Legg Mason have been very kind and helpful. I especially appreciate the time Bill Miller took from his busy schedule to talk with me. Even with all this help, I take full responsibility for the book, and any errors or omissions that may occur are my own.

Introduction

Many of the people mentioned here live and work in New York City. They bravely carried on during one of the most horrific and difficult times in American history: the terrorist attacks on the World Trade Center and the Pentagon on September 11, 2001. Despite their own pain and sorrow, they were very patient with the interruptions this event caused in my life while working on this book. My commendation and sincere thanks to every one of you.

Janet Lowe
Del Mar, California
Fall 2001

CHAPTER 1

BILL MILLER: THE GO-TO GUY FOR NEW ECONOMY VALUE INVESTING

You got to be very careful if you don't know where you're going, because you might not get there.

Yogi Berra

The telephone rings. A young woman hurriedly announces that Bill Miller will be on the line in a second. Is this a good time for the interview? Actually, my computer is down for a couple of hours with my carefully crafted questions inside. But we've tried to arrange this telephone tête-à-tête for weeks. Miller is traveling. I am traveling. Okay, let's go for it. I warn him that I'm taking notes by hand, juggling the telephone and a legal pad, working from memory. Fine. He blasts off like a verbal rocket ship, firing out big concepts, spewing multisyllabic words, responding to questions as if his afterburners are in full tilt.

Whew! William H. Miller III, America's new money master, is a man in a hurry, but he's not showing off, brushing off, or short shrifting. By nature a high-energy, intellectualizing type (what else can you say about a man who uses the word *enantiodromia*—i.e., to proceed by way of opposites, or to swing the other way—in an annual report), Miller has earned celebrity status among investors and his peers by taking a classic concept—value investing—and catapulting it into the twenty-first century.

Michael Mauboussin, an investment strategist at Credit Suisse First Boston who also teaches an investment class at Columbia Business School, considers Miller the best mutual fund manager in America. "He's had a couple of things that land-mined this year (2001). But the guy made more money than God in AOL and Dell."[1] (By 1999, Miller had a 3,500 percent gain in Dell. At that time, he began trimming down his position.)

Fifty-two-year-old Miller runs the Baltimore-based Legg Mason Funds and is manager of the $11.8 billion Value Trust, the only diversified fund to beat the Standard & Poor's 500 for 11 years in a row. He was named Morningstar's Domestic Equity Fund Manager of the Year in 1998 and was his fellow analysts' choice for Morningstar's 1999 Investment Portfolio Manager of the Decade category. For the life of Value Trust, it has given an 18.24 percent annual return, and since 1991 Miller has achieved an annual total return of 18.16 percent, putting him laps ahead of most value-oriented money managers. In his eighth year of outperforming the S&P, he seized the record from former Fidelity Magellan legend Peter Lynch.

Furthermore, Miller achieved these records in a market that was decidedly hostile to value fund managers. For 30 years, from the mid-1960s to the mid-1990s, value was the front-running performance style, but since 1995 value funds have taken second place to growth funds. Some growth managers grouse that Miller only achieved stellar results throughout the 1990s because he abandoned value principles by switching from the old-economy blue-chip companies to a new-economy high-tech mode.

In fact, Miller does, from time to time and for significant parts of his portfolio, journey into the world of contemporary technologies. Yet he says this in no way diminishes his love affair with the fundamental value concepts. It does indicate, however, that Miller sees the future and knows that at some point value investing concepts and the world of high-technology business must meet, greet, and enter into a relationship.

THE RACE FOR THE BETTER BRAIN

Computer scientist Ray Kurzweil, author of *The Age of Spiritual Machines: When Computers Exceed Human Intelligence*, predicts that by the year 2018 computers costing just $1,000 will have roughly the same intelligence as the human brain. They will be able to talk with humans, recognize us, and keep us company when we're lonely. Short of an opposable thumb and a few other features, they'll have everything humans have. And within 10 years more, a $1,000 computer brain will have the power of a thousand human minds. The brilliant machines will start claiming consciousness—the digital equivalent of "I think, therefore I am." Kurzweil writes that "The specter is not yet here." But, he adds, "The emergence in the early 21st century of a new form of intelligence on earth that can compare with, and ultimately exceed that of human intelligence, will be a development of greater import than any of the events that have shaped human history."[2]

Given the potential impact of advances in electronic communication and computerization, can the revolution this implies be ignored by the investment world? Change is coming on galloping hooves, and indeed, investors have been overtaken by change before. But the canniest among them rode with the herd, embracing the onslaught as Bill Miller has done, rather than resisting it.

In their book *Information Rules,* Carl Shapiro, former chief economist to the Justice Department, and Hal R. Varian, dean of the School of Information Management and Systems at University of California–Berkeley, point out that a hundred years ago the way people lived and worked was turned upside down by two early network industries: the electricity grid and the telephone system. The rate of adoption may have been slower than the adoption of the Internet and it took longer for unifying standards to be established, but just as the impact of the Internet is huge, so were electricity and the telephone. Some experts claim that computers and the Internet are nothing more than the next evolutionary stage of these seminal technologies. Whatever the case, one thing is clear: Information technology is no longer something that nerds manipulate for kicks; it has become big business. Those who avoid it risk being left behind.

CAUGHT IN THE CORRECTION

Yet, as everyone discovered as the millennium dawned, high-kicking high tech is as risky as the old fuddy-duddies warned. And despite his innovative meshing of high tech and value, Miller to some extent got caught in the correction. Like all investors, he has chosen dynamite and duds, held both losers and winners too long, and simply missed the message on some superior companies. Like Warren Buffett and other longtime survivors in the investment world, Miller has occasional down ticks. During the late 1980s, Value Trust underperformed 4 out of 5 years, and ratings from Morningstar and other ratings services were an embarrassment. Although Miller turned that around and continued to outperform the S&P 500 through the end of the twentieth century and into the twenty-first, the returns on his funds were sometimes in negative percentages. Fortunately, the S&P's negatives were greater than Value Trust's. But Miller says these occasional slumps don't matter. Ten good years in a row "cuts you a lot of slack. I can underperform this year, next, for the next 3 years really."

All this said, those irritating, tenacious, value-oriented questions remain: When information technology stocks have such limited histories, how can an investor be certain that revenues will grow, free cash flow will be strong, and other fundamentals will materialize? With the wispy information that is usually available, how can anyone figure out whether a company's price is too much or too little? Miller admits he doesn't always know for sure. And his critics have expressed doubts at times that he is sure of what he's doing.

In fact, that's not even the way Miller thinks about his investments. He is acutely aware that in the investment world, there is no such thing as certainty. It's all about probability—how probable is it that a stock will achieve an expected return over time? Miller fully expects to be wrong a certain number of times, but he expects to be so spectacularly right enough times that he will achieve a high level of performance. For example, explains one of his analysts, Mark Niemann, if Miller is investing in four companies, three of them might go to zero. But if the fourth went to 6 times its current price, Miller could end up with a 50 percent return, or a total return on his portfolio that would beat the market. In fact, an analysis of Miller's portfolio performance would show that he sometimes has a lower frequency of correct picks than other managers do, although his return remains high.

"I USED TO BE SNOW WHITE, BUT I DRIFTED"—MAE WEST

Imagine the uproar in the mid-1990s when Bill Miller, a conservative-type money manager from Baltimore, started nosing around tech stocks, then made the big leap—God forbid—to telecommunications and Internet issues.

To a whole crowd of observers, old-line Legg Mason Wood Walker Inc.'s Value Trust, which eventually had 20 percent of its assets in stocks such as America Online, Amazon.com, and Dell Computers, was a travesty. To many, Value Trust, always a blend of value and growth, had crossed the line to become a growth fund. After all, it now quacked and waddled and flapped its wings like a growth fund. So a growth fund it must be.

"Lots of value managers, like William Miller at Legg Mason Value, are no longer buying what we consider value stocks," wrote mutual fund columnist Mary Rowland. "Miller's record is great, with annual returns of more than 43 percent over the last three years. But is it value, when your top holdings including America Online, Dell Computer, and MCI WorldCom? I don't think so."[3]

Even more critical was a column published in July 1998 on the financial web site theStreet.com. The site's founder, James J. Cramer,

9

wrote, "value in this world has simply become a masquerade, a mean spirited marketing tactic that lures people in the door who would otherwise have no desire to own such nosebleed stocks."

WAS VALUE INVESTING DEAD, OR JUST OUT COLD?

The implications were abundantly clear. Bill Miller had become a poseur, a pretender—no longer a crew-cut, establishment-value guy. What's more, if a man smart enough to beat the S&P 500 year in and year out was jumping ship, then clearly value was dead. Journalists were among those who shouted the loudest that Miller had sold his very soul, especially those writers who pinned their analysis on highly simplified investment definitions.

Most of the pooh-poohing of Miller as a value investor came in the late 1990s, when respectable publications were happily and confidently chiseling headstones for the value approach. In an article typical of the times, *Businessweek* reported that despite the new-millennium revival of the classic approach, "the current rally could also be the last hurrah for old-style value investing. Such investing produces its best results in a traditional business cycle. Value stocks typically achieve most of their gains from the bottom of a recession to the top of the expansion as the rising economic tide lifts revenues and profits. Growth stocks—those with more reliable earnings streams—then outperform value stocks in the down phase of the business cycle.

"In a period of declining profits, the market prizes the companies whose earnings can continue to grow. But now, thanks to technology, globalization, and a savvier monetary policy, the business cycle has been dampened and elongated. From 1945 to 1991, the U.S. economy went through nine recessions. The current expansion is eight years old [this was in 1999], with no recession in sight. With fewer recessions, there are fewer opportunities for typical value stocks to shine. Low inflation also works against value investing."[4]

THE VETERAN SLUGGERS

Could the furor surrounding value have occurred because a generation raised on instant gratification couldn't deal with value-specific time frames? In fact, over extended periods of 20 years or more, value invariably beats growth. From 1946 to 2000, according to the research firm Ibbotson, value stocks bested growth stocks 15.4 percent to 11.5 percent. Put another way, $100 invested in value stocks in 1946 would have been worth $266,544 by 2001, compared to only $39,681 for growth stocks. Yet go back only 5 years, to 1996, and growth and value dash forward in a dead heat, with a 15.3 percent annualized increase for growth and a 15.1 percent rise in value securities. It only takes 10 years for value to overtake growth; by then, value has a 15.4 percent annual increase and growth stocks have slipped to 14.6 percent.[5]

Those who accused Miller of changing his stripes seemed insufficiently aware that the mission, the aspiration, the dream of value investors is to buy stocks that show the promise of growth. Clearly, all investors share this goal—to buy something now that will be worth more later. But value investors only want these stocks when they can be snatched up at a price comfortably beneath their intrinsic, or true, value. Given some of his choices, it was difficult for cynical observers to imagine Miller in the company of other great, revered, enduring value investors such as the late Columbia University professor and author Benjamin Graham, Warren Buffett of Berkshire Hathaway, William Ruane of the Sequoia Fund, Sir John Templeton of the Templeton Funds, or John Neff, retired from Windsor Funds. And, in fact, Miller doesn't exactly fit that mold. The difference between the various value practitioners—then and now—is how they make their choices and how long they're willing to wait for rewards.

Money manager and author, Robert Hagstrom, says that among investment gurus Miller has much in common with Buffett's curmudgeonly partner, Charlie Munger, who spent his early investment years combing every possible investment situation, shopping for bargains and overlooked possibilities. Later, Munger changed his approach. He decided deep value purchases took too much time to come to fruition, caused too much psychic pain. Better to pay a little more for solid value and sleep well at night without fears that your big investment might flip belly up.

GROWTH VERSUS VALUE

Even writers who should have known better were befuddled by Miller's approach because while they admired his accomplishments, they felt they couldn't find an easy niche for him. *Barron's* described Miller as an investment manager to whom "the investment muse speaks in a mysterious fashion, and one that has led him both to excellent results and a style that resists categorization."[6]

Nevertheless, perhaps due to his years of studying philosophy, Miller is sanguine about being misunderstood.

"I attribute it to the inability of people to understand long-term investing. 'Growth' and 'value' are labels that people use to try to categorize things," he said. "If you look at Morningstar's investment-style grid, we have migrated through the whole spectrum. Yet this fund has invested the same way for 15 years."[7]

From its inception in 1982 to 2001, Legg Mason Value Trust has had an average annual total return of 18.24 percent. Originally Miller managed the fund under the tutelage of respected veteran money manager Ernie Kiehne. Even with its admirable return, Value Trust had underperformed the market 4 out of 5 years in the late 1980s. This included two separate 2-year periods. "Those were years of greater economic volatility than we have experienced recently, as the more cyclical parts of the economy swung from periods of strength to weakness and investor behavior alternated between euphoria (1986 to mid-1987) and panic (late 1987 and 1990). During that period, the world was rocked by the collapse of oil prices in 1986, the dollar's weakness and the federal reserve's raising of interest rates in 1987, the fall of communism in 1989, the savings and loan banking crisis in 1989 and 1990, and the invasion of Kuwait in 1990, which sent oil prices spiraling up."[8]

Then in 1990 Miller took charge. Luckily, that year Wall Street was entering into its most remarkable growth phase ever. But even on top of that, Miller, as we shall see, supercharged the fund's performance. Between 1991 and 2001, the fund gave investors an average annual return of 21.05 percent.

Despite the fact that Value Trust outpaced the S&P 500 for 10 years in a row, Miller went through a frighteningly difficult streak in 2000. His fund trailed the S&P that January and February, due mainly to weakness in one of his core holdings, AOL. Investors began fleeing the fund at a clip of $20 million a day. Nevertheless, Miller managed that year again to best the S&P 500. We'll examine his record and review the lessons learned later in this chapter.

What has enabled Miller to weather so many financial storms? The *New York Times* asserted in early 2001 that it's his consistency that has made him "the reluctant, rumpled star of the investment world."[9] Despite his willingness to dive into the technology sector, Miller's personal style resembles that of the stodgy value crowd rather than the cocky, high-energy, reactive managers so often associated with tech funds.[10]

MILLER'S DEFINITION OF VALUE

And what *is* the style of the nation's mutual fund champion? Miller explains:

"W*e try to buy companies that trade at large discounts to intrinsic value. What's different is we will look for that value anywhere we can. We don't rule out technology as an area to look for value.*"[11]

Then Miller drives his main point home:

"Our definition of value comes directly from the finance textbooks, which define value for any investment as the present value of the future free cash flows of that investment. You will not find value defined in terms of low P/E [price-to-earnings] or low price–to–cash flow in the finance literature. What you find is that practicing investors use those metrics as a proxy for potential bargain-priced stocks. Sometimes they are and sometimes they aren't."[12]

What, finally and decisively, earns for Miller the crown of a value investor, even though he sometimes seems to break all the traditional rules by buying short-history stocks with extremely high price-to-equity ratios?

- Like the purist Graham, Miller ignores the fickle moods of the infamous Mr. Market. "I don't have a strong view of the overall market," says Miller. "There is very little value added trying to predict where the market is going or guessing whether it's overpriced or underpriced," he says.[13]
- Like value icon Buffett, Miller looks for franchise value. This is one of the characteristics he likes about Amazon.com.
- Like John Burr Williams, Miller is willing to forecast when he runs the numbers. At the same time, he believes that numbers aren't enough to tell you everything you need to know before dialing up your brokerage firm and placing an order to buy a stock.
- Like Charlie Munger, Miller looks for investment ideas everywhere.

- Like all value investors, when making stock purchases, Miller works a margin of safety into his calculations. There is room for error. "Our methods are designed to try and capture companies very early on in their potential return stage, meaning they've been beaten down," he explains.[14]

- Like Sequoia Fund's William Ruane, Miller is not a frequent trader. He buys and holds; he invests for the long term.[15] "I'll easily trade no rate of return in the near term for higher confidence that the stock will outperform in the long term," he says.[16]

BUCKING THE TREND

To be sure, Miller took the majority of his criticism when the value approach to investing was in one of its most difficult phases. Value always suffers at the top of a bull market, but the situation looked especially bad in the summer of 2000. That year, Mark Coffelt, whose Texas Capital Value & Growth Fund had one of the lowest P/Es in its class, said, "Value has had what is the equivalent of a 200-year flood."[17]

Although Coffelt conceded that the last 2 years of the century were the worst in nearly 50 years for pilgrims in search of low-P/E stocks, he promised that value investing was due for a comeback and should do better than the so-called growth stocks over the first 5 years of the new millennium. "We don't think the laws of physics have changed," Coffelt said.[18]

In the enigmatic way of Wall Street, while the death knell was still ringing for value investing, certain value investors—Miller among them—were knocking down the blocks. In early 2000 Mohnish Pabrai, founder of the Pabrai Investment Fund I (PIFI), was beating more than 99 percent of mutual funds and professional fund managers. His PIFI, which is modeled after Warren Buffett's first partnership (which was formed in the late 1950s and disbanded in the early 1970s), had a 62.5 percent return (before fees and expenses) and outperformed all three market indices: the Dow Jones Industrial Average by 68.7 percent, the S&P 500 by 57.8 percent, and the NASDAQ Composite by 15.2 percent. Pabrai is an ardent value disciple and yet certainly managed his affairs differently from Miller. "Our performance is very compelling for the year because it was achieved by buying very mundane stuff," Pabrai said. "We have made very little in terms of pure technology bets. I'm only interested in investing in companies where I can project at least 5 to 10 years forward—by definition this is virtually impossible with most technology companies."[19]

Miller admitted the following year that his style might be open to criticism, but still, it got the job done:

> "*Over the long term [LM Value Trust] has provided shareholders with very attractive returns. However, along the way to this long-term outperformance, the fund has seen numerous quarters of under performance. Performance history suggests that periods of market weakness can be excellent opportunities for investment.*"[20]

As might be expected, when tech's winning streak ended, value stocks again became the champions. The rush back to value, with its reputation for safety, began, and mutual fund investors were swift to move. Bill Nygren's Oakmark Select Fund, which had $3.1 billion in assets, gained significantly in the first 4 months of 2001. Nygren was so alarmed by the sudden $700 million in hot money that he stopped accepting new investors early in May. He feared that size would make it impossible to stick to the successful strategy of owning only 20 stocks and investing in midsized companies. Additionally, "There's a concern that many of our new investors are performance chasers who could be disruptive to the fund," Nygren explained.[21] Because investors perceived Value Trust as a tech-heavy fund, however, just the opposite happened to Miller. Investors withdrew.

Nevertheless, the resurgence in investor confidence was encouraging to those who stubbornly called themselves value investors. "Market action over the past year confirms that valuation does matter," said Miller.[22]

DO WHAT THE ALL-STARS DO

All the great enduring investors have been value investors. Joining Graham, Buffett, Templeton, and Neff on the value honor roll are Mario J. Gabelli of the Gabelli Funds; Bill Nygren, mentioned earlier, of Oakmark Select Fund; Mason Hawkins, founder of Longleaf Partners; and Larry Sondike of Mutual Shares. Table 1.1 below shows the performance of each of these managers over the past year and since the funds' creation.

Although these investors share a fundamental philosophy, each of them has created his own interpretation of classical value. Early on, Gabelli began valuing companies for the cash they generate rather than their assets or earnings. That concept became the tool used by corporate raiders during the leveraged-buyout boom of the 1980s.

Table 1.1

Fund Manager	1 year %	10 years %	Since Inception (annualized) (%)	Since Inception (cumulative) (%)
Legg Mason Value Trust/Miller	−13.68	18.49	18.17	2488.78
Oakmark Select/Nygren	33.73	NA	29.04	252.46
Longleaf Partners/Hawkins	−2.77	16.80	14.73	633.84
Gabelli Value Fund/Gabelli	−5.83	16.42	14.05	386.46
Mutual Shares Fund/Sondike	−4.16	NA	13.08	232.45

Investors came up with the term *private market value* to designate the price a savvy investor would pay for the entire company. Deal makers bought heavily into companies they saw as undervalued and then used the company's own cash to pay down the money borrowed to finance the purchase. Or at least that was the stated goal. All too often, however, the debt was left unpaid, a dragging anchor on the acquired unit's performance.[23]

As for Buffett, leveraged buyouts have never been his game, but he also stretched the traditional value style when in 1988 Berkshire Hathaway Inc. grabbed a $600 million stake in Coca-Cola, and in 1989 a $600 million position in Gillette Co. (in 1989, Buffett increased his Coca-Cola position to $1.2 billion). At the time, neither company was viewed as value stock, and the price seemed unnaturally high for Buffett. But he'd learned from his partner and vice chairman, Charlie Munger, that the old "cigar butt" style of value investing had risks of its own. Often, these deep value buys were badly battered operations. It took time, and sometimes additional cash, to coax these deep/cheap stocks back up to sell for full value. How much more pleasant to pay a higher price, get an appreciated global franchise, and enjoy the long and relatively easy ride up. By 2001, Berkshire's Coca-Cola stake was worth $9.4 billion and its Gillette shares were worth $2.8 billion.

THE MAN WHO COACHED MILLER

Miller had been introduced to value investing concepts in college, but it was Ernie Kiehne, a lively octogenarian and the cofounder of Value Trust, who really indoctrinated Miller into the value way. Miller, Chip Mason, and Kiehne share a love of baseball, each of them having played for their school teams in their youths. Kiehne, a natty dresser from the old school, has long favored the traditional value stocks such as banks, General Motors, and Citicorp (now Citigroup). Miller says he still manages money in a way very similar to that of his mentor, except that Kiehne—who incidentally still serves on Miller's investment team—is more traditional. In what way? "I rely a little more on modern portfolio theory," says Miller. "And we've become much more sophisticated in our valuation methods."[24] (We focus on these advanced valuation methods in future chapters.)

Miller's formation was far from the B-school track. A native of Florida, he graduated with honors from Washington and Lee University in Lexington, Virginia, in 1972, earning an undergraduate degree in European history and economics. After a stint as an Army intelligence officer, Miller pursued a doctorate in philosophy—more specifically, legal and political ethics—at Johns Hopkins University. "So I have not been infected by business school misinformation," he says with a wry grin. "I have my own propri etary source of misinformation."[25]

Miller considered teaching philosophy at one point, but took his professors seriously when they forewarned his class that there were no teaching jobs out there to be had. If the students had no fundamental fascination with the discipline, they might as well study something else. Miller stuck with philosophy through the end of the course work, but stopped short of writing a doctoral dissertation.

This was largely because he'd become increasingly fascinated with financial matters. Michael Hooker, who taught philosophy at Johns Hopkins when Miller studied there, recalls arriving for work each morning: "I was the first faculty member to get to work, and when I would arrive, Bill would be sitting in the faculty library reading The *Wall Street Journal.*" Hooker encouraged Miller to give up philosophy and try his hand at finance instead.

This led to a job in the mid-1970s as a financial officer and later treasurer at the manufacturing company J.E.Baker Co.[26] The York, Pennsylvania–based company operates quarries from which it produces dolomite products, to be used primarily in the production of steel and cement. Miller was overseer of some of J.E. Baker's investment portfolios, and discovered it was the part of the job he enjoyed the most.

During his stint at Baker, Miller's wife, Leslie, who he met and married in 1974 when he was in the Army, was working at Legg Mason as a broker and assistant to the financial house's star broker, Harry Ford. Miller would come by in the afternoon to pick her up from work, and while waiting, start digging through the company's research reports. Raymond "Chip" Mason, Legg Mason's chairman, recalls that Miller would show up about 4:30, and at 6:30 when his wife was ready to leave, he would be so immersed in research reports that Leslie would have to prod him to go.

Leslie Miller introduced her husband to Kiehne, then the firm's head of research. As luck would have it, Kiehne and Mason had launched a search for a person to replace Kiehne as he planned for his eventual retirement. It was somewhat of a surprise to Kiehne to realize he'd met the best possible candidate standing by the water cooler, but with fewer than 500 employees Legg Mason was a relatively small organization and Miller's fascination with research had attracted attention. Miller was hired at the century-old firm in 1981 and a few years later became Kiehne's successor.

Legg Mason remains a relatively small firm, although it has become highly regarded and is quickly strengthening as a global player. With approximately $175 billion under management, it ranks as the 25th largest money manager in the United States.

▰▰▰   THE WINNING TEAM

As chief executive officer of Legg Mason Funds Management, Inc., Miller is responsible for five investment mutual funds valued at about $23 billion, including individually managed accounts and large institutional accounts. He also manages two funds at Legg Mason: the Value Trust and the Opportunity Trust. Additionally, he's one of the elite, outside team managers of Master Select Equity Fund, an experimental fund in which mutual fund newsletter publisher Ken Gregory is trying out out some of his ideas.

Until 2001, Miller had managed the Special Investment Trust as well, but that year it was taken over by Lisa Rapuano, age 36, one of the brain trust babies on Miller's 12-member research team and three traders. The Special Investment Trust follows the same investment strategy as Value Trust, but mostly operates in a different market segment—small-and mid-sized companies. About 25 percent of the fund is invested in special situations or corporate turnarounds. Under Miller's guidance, the Special Investment Trust had a solidly good record, outperforming its benchmark, the Russell 2000, by 960 basis points over the 5-year period ending December 31, 1999. Over its full 16-year life, the trust has had a 14.4 percent average annual total return. With this $2 billion fund, Miller invested principally in common stocks of smaller, out-of-favor companies involved in restructurings or other special situations. While these companies have the alluring growth potential of deep value buys, they also carry extra risk, not to mention the possibility of extremely long workout periods. With 42 percent of its assets in technology (at the peak in March), the fund limped through 2000 with a negative 17.74 percent return. The only consolation for shareholders was that the Special Investment Trust did better than its benchmark S&P 400 index, a minus 21.6 between March 2000 and March 2001. By that time the fund had outperformed its benchmark six consecutive years.

But Miller's blazing star remains Value Trust, which seeks growth of capital by purchasing securities that appear to be undervalued in relation to the earning power or asset value of the company. As the prospectus coyly states, "the fund is marketed to investors who seek capital growth in an effort to combat inflation." At the end of 2000, Nancy Dennin, who has worked with Miller for more than a decade, became assistant portfolio manager of Value Trust. Although her record has been excellent overall, Dennin for a time managed Legg Mason Total Return, which was not one of the company's stellar funds and since has been folded into another fund.

PLAY BY PLAY

Value Trust was established on April 23, 1982, with a beginning net asset value of $10 per share. It was a nerve-wracking time to launch a new fund, with double-digit interest rates that severely impacted the stock market. The Dow Jones Industrial Average stood at 825, off 19

21

percent from its April 1981 bull market high of 1,024. Two months after it started, the fund had 331 shareholders with net assets of $1.1 million and a net asset value of $10.25 per share.

In the first 10 years of Value Trust's history, Miller and Kiehne were comanagers of the fund. Even though the 1980s were generally good for value stocks, Value Trust generated mixed results. Kiehne was a classicist with affection for blue-chip low-P/E stocks. He expressed a liking for bank stocks, but initially at least, only 40 percent of the fund's total assets were in stocks. Stocks were a relatively small part of the portfolio at first because Kiehne and Miller were building their positions slowly over time, a process known at Legg Mason as "munching." Professional investors like to munch at a stock so as not to influence its market price. A sudden, large block purchase could drive the price unnaturally higher. Among the holdings were American Cyanamid, American Telephone and Telegraph, Norfolk Southern Companies, and Westinghouse Electric Corporation. The fund surged in the first few years after its inception. It then lagged for a few years, and when the market tumbled in 1990, bank stocks were among the biggest losers.[27] (For a full list of the fund's holdings at that time, see page 167.)

In 1990, with Value Trust facing a 17 percent decline, Kiehne turned the reins over to Miller. Despite difficult times and lackluster performance since 1986, there were well over 2,000 shareholders in the fund and net asset value per share had increased to $26.76. Even before he saw what was happening to the fund's cache of bank stocks, Miller was shifting toward a more flexible definition of value, relying on future cash flow, return on equity, and other measures that Buffett and other individualistic value investors were already pioneering.[28]

Within the year, Value Trust was beating the S&P 500, 35 percent to 30 percent, but not without an ironic twist: The fund got its greatest boost from Kiehne's reviving bank stocks, as well as other traditional plays such as Fannie Mae, Philip Morris, and the insurer, Orion Capital.[29] "I made a lot of mistakes," reflects Kiehne, "but some of them turned out all right anyway."[30]

Miller did well, but he told shareholders in his 1993 annual report that someone else did better, or at least would have if he was managing investments. "The first quarter belonged to Bill Clinton, who undoubtedly would have been the best performing money manager in America if only those pesky conflict of interest rules were not around. The stocks he likes: autos, airlines, energy, and especially natural gas, did wonderfully; but the ones he did not like: profiteering health care companies, the sinful alcoholic beverage and tobacco stocks, the gluttonous foods, were horrid. Bonds, which he loves, soared and carried stocks with them."[31]

What sounded like praise for Clinton turned the opposite direction at the end of that same report. "Bonds rose sharply in the first quarter and the administration was too quick to conclude the markets were ratifying its policies or, more accurately, proposals," Miller wrote, then added, "Despite the administration's glee at them, rising bond prices are not portents of prosperity. Bond holders are happiest during depressions."[32]

That same year, Miller met with John Reed, chief executive officer of Citicorp, which led him to establish a new position in the stock. Citicorp, America's largest bank, had a dreadful long-term history, and was selling for less than it had in 1929. But, explained Miller, in the course of their conversations it became apparent that Reed "had finally embraced cost control and the idea that the bank is in business to earn a return for its owners. It has an unparalleled global franchise and we expect earnings to approach $4 per share next year."[33]

Near the end of 1993, Miller's race with the S&P was running neck and neck. Value Trust trailed behind the S&P 500 right into the final weeks of the year. Miller remained anxiously hopeful that the fund would be "the horse that comes from the back to win by a nose," and his wish was granted. The last-minute burst of speed came from late gains by RJR Nabisco Holdings and Humana.[34]

The rising interest rates in 1994 again beleaguered the fund's bank stocks. To make the picture even darker, an out-of-the-blue devaluation of the Mexican peso battered the Mexican stocks in Value Trust—Grupo Financiero Serfin and Teléfonos de Mexico. "Judging by the market's action in the past two months, investors began the first quarter unaware of two things they were fully cognizant of by the quarter's end: stocks do not react well to rapidly rising interest rates and Mexico is not the fifty-first state,"[35] Miller wrote. But again, the portfolio got an unexpected, last-minute push when Caesar's World leaped 20 percent as the result of an acquisition bid by ITT Corp. Value Trust finished the year seven-hundredths of a percentage point ahead of the S&P 500.[36]

THE MENTAL GAME OF INVESTING

The most impressive advances to the fund came in 1996, about the time Miller discovered a source of inspiration at the cerebral Santa Fe Institute. Under the influence of economists and scientists meeting in the "city different," as Santa Fe calls itself, Miller experienced an intellectual awakening. (The nature and impact of Santa Fe's new-age theoretics is discussed in Chapter 2.) He considered investing in depressed paper companies, as certain other value investors were doing, or buying Dell, which was cheap because of worries over a cyclical downturn in PC sales. Because of some of the business leaders he talked to Miller concluded that the PC industry would, in time, become a commodity business with a few large players dominating. He figured Dell, a low-cost producer, would be among the leaders. The stock skyrocketed almost immediately after he bought Dell, which helped Value Trust whomp the S&P 500 by 15 percentage points that year.[37]

Based on similar reasoning, Miller started acquiring shares in the Internet access provider, America Online. In 1997, AOL shares rose 172 percent and Dell climbed 216 percent, driving Value Trust 37 percent higher. Although their prices were soaring, Miller did not cut back on those stocks as he might have in the past. He stuck with a winning hand. The holdings continued to multiply many times over and ballooned into a large portion of Value Trust's portfolio.[38]

About this same time, Miller became concerned that the stock market was overheated. As he put it in his 1997 *Legg Mason Annual*

Report, "We believe that the period of extraordinary stock returns that began in 1982 ended in 1996. Valuations are too high and future growth rates too low for stocks to average more than 9 or 10 percent per year."[39] He reached this conclusion because although corporate earnings growth was solid, pricing power had evaporated, unemployment was low—putting pressure on wages—and corporate profit margins were high by historical standards. Miller said the best possible rate an investor should expect, long term, was between 9 and 10 percent. "Sensitive investors will be prepared for periods, perhaps extended, where returns are well below those levels, or even negative."[40] Because his thinking was in fact premature, Miller picked up the entire passage from his 1997 report and repeated it word for word in the 1998 missive.

THE STANDARD & POOR'S HIDDEN MAP

At the close of 1999, the *Wall Street Journal* claimed that Miller was taking cues from the S&P 500 index itself. The index, overseen by McGraw-Hill Co.'s Standard & Poor's unit, said the *Wall Street Journal* "occasionally replaces lackluster businesses with better ones but mostly lets its winners ride." That is an inexact description of what Miller was thinking, especially since the purpose of any index is to reflect the reality of a particular market, not to outpace it. However, since the S&P—the broadest of all indices—was beating such a hot path, it made sense to pay attention to those stocks that were stoking the S&P fire. (More about the S&P strategy in Chapter 4.) Suffice it to say that Miller eventually let AOL shares rise to 19 percent of his portfolio and technology stocks to increase to a total of 41 percent of assets. He trimmed his AOL position only slightly in early 1999, even though he then considered the stock overvalued.[41]

In the summer of 1999, AOL and other Internet stocks tumbled head-over-heels. Value Trust's lead over its benchmark eroded from more than 15 percentage points in April to less than 1 percentage point in September. The pain eased at the end of the year, however, when the tech sector recovered. That year, Value Trust again scored big with AOL. Miller also triumphed with the help of holdings in cell-phone manufacturer Nokia, computer maker Gateway, and global advertising giant WPP Group.

In late 1999, Miller invested in Amazon.com, which the *Wall Street Journal* described as his most audacious move thus far. The Internet retailer had suffered a series of financial losses, to which the market overreacted. By the end of 1999, the stock was trading at about 22 times its expected 1999 sales. Yet Miller believed Amazon had achieved a virtually unassailable lead in its own business sector. It would be able to grow enormously, even without massive capital infusions and the debt or dilution of shares that often attends growth.

RETURN TO A TRADITIONAL STRATEGY

Despite the promise of many of his high-tech acquisitions, Miller attempted to bring balance to his holdings by buying Waste Management, Kroger supermarkets, and the toy maker, Mattel. (A detailed account of the Waste Management acquisition is in Chapter 7.)

But again, in mid-December 2000, Miller seemed to have fallen into a slump. "It's a very hostile investing environment out there," Miller observed. "Last year, over 127 funds were up over 100 percent. So investors ask: What are you guys doing? You are in the wrong stuff. You are missing the easy money."[42]

At an analyst's presentaton at New York's "21" Club in late 2000, Miller projected a Calvin & Hobbes cartoon strip showing 6-year-old Calvin saying, "How can something seem so plausible at the time and so idiotic in retrospect?" as a water balloon explodes in his hands.

"That's the way I feel with a lot of stocks we bought this year," said Miller. "The three names we bought last year all collapsed; the ones we bought this year collapsed." So, he joked, "I think we'll buy none next year."[43]

TAKING FLIGHT

Investors began fleeing Value Trust even before it paid out $7.82 a share in taxable gain on December 22, 2000. Some of them did so with Miller's blessing. A month before, Miller warned the fund's directors that all shareholders who had been in the fund less than a year should sell out. That way, most of them could take the losses on their income tax returns and avoid receiving the gain, which would be taxable. The gains were earned by selling stock, but the benefits had accrued to earlier investors in the fund. By that mid-December, money was gushing out at as much as $20 million a day, and the fund's assets had diminished by $1.5 billion from its peak of $13.7 billion.

At that moment, with less than 3 weeks left in the year, Value Trust was running dead even with the S&P 500. Value Trust had fallen far behind the market earlier in 2000, as dot.coms and other technology stocks were rocketing. Miller was able to regain an edge over the S&P when he sold chunks of AOL and some other winners, and reverting to Kiehne's old favorites, again purchased lagging financial stocks, Citigroup and Fannie Mae. Another pleasant surprise was Waste Management, which gained nearly 60 percent for the year.

It was only in the last weeks of 2000 that Miller began to gain a slight lead on the S&P 500. Miller celebrated Christmas in Santa Fe with his family, but checked on progress regularly. With only 3 trading days left in the year, Value Trust was down 8.1 percent compared to a 9.5 decline in the S&P. The following day, December 28, Value Trust had a strong day, and the lead seemed secure. The final score: Value Trust lost only 7.14 percent, beating the S&P 500 by 2 percentage points. Miller returned to his office after the first of the year to find it decorated with banners. The investment team celebrated with a catered lunch of sushi, followed by cake and champagne. But, Miller wryly noted that people were being strangely appreciative, considering that the fund lost money for the year.

It was the tenth year that Miller bested the benchmark. His

fund's return would have been 10 to 20 percentage points worse than that of the market had he not taken the portfolio actions that he did.[44] By the end of 2001 Miller pulled another rabbit out of the hat and outperformed the S&P 500 eleven years in a row.

TECHNOLOGY TIPS THE SCALES

Miller later reported to shareholders:

> "*I*nvestment success in both 1999 and 2000 was determined almost exclusively by how heavily weighted one was in technology. In 1999, the tech-heavy NASDAQ rose 85 percent, the largest single increase of any broad-based market index in U.S. history. In 2000, that index fell 39 percent, its worst showing ever. Managers who were overweight in the TMT area (tech, media, and telecom) had a great 1999 and a terrible 2000."[45]

OPPORTUNITY TRUST

Miller launched his brainchild, the Opportunity Trust, in December 1999—an inauspicious time. Miller's plan for the fund was to invest in selected companies using the valuation tool he developed in his other funds, multifactor valuation analysis. Miller analyzes a company's share price using a range of value measures, then looks at the distribution of the results. The distribution gives him a clearer idea of the appropriate valuation. This "go-anywhere" portfolio would hold stocks that had been identified as priced at a significant discount to their intrinsic values, be they large or small, domestic or foreign. The fund, said Jennifer Murphy, chief operating officer for Legg Mason Fund Management, is "not intended to be guided by any investment style." Miller cautioned that the fund has been designed for investors comfortable with the risk inherent in an aggressively managed fund, and that turnover in the portfolio could be extremely high. As it turns out, this has been a fund for patient people with patient money. Opportunity Trust outperformed its benchmark index initially, then spent months and months under water before rising to the surface. Since its revival in 2000, it has achieved a 10.25 percent average annual return, measured from the fund's inception. For the first half of 2001, Opportunity had a return of 18.36 percent.

One of the drawbacks to the fund is its annual expense ratio, a rather hefty 1.98 percent. On an average, actively managed diversified funds have an expense ratio of 1.47 percent.[46] Value Trust's expense ratio of 1.69 percent is also more expensive than most other mutual funds.

MASTERS' SELECT EQUITY FUND

In addition to handling his Legg Mason funds, Miller is one of the team managers of Ken Gregory's Masters' Select Equity Fund.

Gregory, who runs the advisory firm of Littman/Gregory and publishes the *No-Load Fund Analyst* newsletter, went public with the innovative concept behind Masters' Select in December 1996. Six top managers were chosen, representing the spectrum from growth to value to large-cap stocks to small-cap stocks. The idea was to create a core equity portfolio built to outperform through the rolling waves of market cycles. From the start it was recognized that Masters' Select Equity might never be the number 1 performer in any given year. It would be judged in terms of a longer, more encouraging and forgiving time frame.

The original Masters' managers were Christopher Davis of Davis

Select Advisers, Foster Friess of Friess Associations, Mason Hawkins of Longleaf Partners, Sig Segalas of Harbor Capital, Dick Weiss of Strong Funds, and deep value manager Robert Sanborn. In 2000, Bill Miller replaced Sanborn.

These are worthy partners for Miller. During the 19 years ending December 31, 1998, for example, Mason Hawkins's Longleaf posted a compound return of 19.5 percent per year versus 17.7 percent per year for the S&P 500 and 14.8 percent per year for the Ibbotson Small Company Index during the same period. For the first 6 months of 2001, the fund had a return of 10.9 percent.

Despite the lineup, this is not team management in the way you might imagine. The managers do not cooperate together in the usual sense. They do not act as a board, getting together, planning strategy, and making investment decisions by consensus—nothing even close to the town council or the school board. Instead, the fund's assets are apportioned among the six "talents," and each is asked to select only his or her top picks.

Each manager contributes 8 to 15 of his best ideas. These can include small-cap stocks because of the fund's relatively small $56 million asset base per manager. Each of these men handle much larger funds on their own. Masters' Select Equity started slowly in late 2000, but gained momentum. It suffered in 2000, partly because of Miller's sizable losses in personal computer–related stocks such as Gateway. The fund's fortunes improved in 2001, but the main contributor to that was not an original Miller pick, but Toys "R" Us, which gained 43 percent in the first 3 months of the year. (More about this valuable holding in Chapter 7.) In time, Miller did, however, invest Legg Mason Funds in Toys "R" Us. The company became a favorite with many value managers.

Masters' Select stock pickers can easily be described as price conscious, and indeed in the year 2000, the $450 million fund outpaced the relevant indexes and most stock funds, a year when the large indexes deflated like a punctured balloon. Though the fund's returns have been positive, at 10.19 percent average annual return the last 3 years of the 20th century, performance has not made the investor's hearts race.

STEP ASIDE, ROCK STARS

Thanks to his wisdom as a stock picker, Miller has become a hero within his own company. "He is our go-to guy," says John Gallagher, a senior Legg Mason broker. "I mean, I used to go to [Rolling] Stones concerts all the time in my younger days, but I will tell you this: I'd rather spend a few minutes with Bill Miller than Mick Jagger."[47]

All this reverence comes at a price. Miller admits he is obsessive about his work. He puts in 7 days a week at the job. His 22nd-floor office looks down on Baltimore Harbor, but even with the sweeping view, the operation has a tight-knit, insular atmosphere. Aside from his wife, two teenage sons, season tickets for a seat behind home plate to the Baltimore Orioles, and his involvement at the Santa Fe Institute, Miller has few interests outside of reading and his work. He is an avid reader and is always recommending books to his coworkers. His briefcase might hold a biography of an obscure philosopher or a paperback edition of *Lives of the Poets*, a 992-page history of English-language poetry, or *At Home in the Universe*, by theoretical biologist Stuart Kauffman. "I don't have any hobbies, like building model airplanes or things like that," admits Miller. Single-minded, he sometimes even reads research reports between innings at Orioles games.[48]

Miller enjoys the perks of success. He drives a Mercedes S500, owns three homes including an 80-acre waterfront estate in Maine, and enjoys the use of a seven-seater Lear 60 jet that costs $2,500 per hour of flying time. And yet the Silicon Valley economist Brian Arthur, a leading Santa Fe Institute theorist and personal friend of Miller, describes him as an unassuming guy. "His main characteristic is curiosity. He just exudes the impression that he is a very decent guy. He will walk into a room and just stand there quietly observing the people. He's interested in everything, everybody."

Arthur says that he's wondered why Miller, with his academic tendencies, devotes hours each day to investment questions, but it is Arthur's opinion that Miller doesn't do it solely to make money. He does it as an intellectual excercise, enjoying it as a challenging mental puzzle. He says that Miller sees the whole picture, understands the basic economics, and won't be sold a bill of goods of any type.[49]

Arthur once asked Miller why he earned his living as a mutual fund manager despite his doctoral studies in philosophy. Miller replied that he wasn't an investor despite his grounding in philosophy; he was intrigued with money management precisely because of his exposure to the discipline of thought. Thanks to that training, says Miller, "I can smell a bad argument miles away."

CHAPTER 2

A WAY OF THINKING

Baseball is 90 percent mental, the other half is physical.

Yogi Berra

Benjamin Graham, who is known as the father of value investing, used to admonish his graduate students at Columbia University's business school to think clearly, and to think independently. No acting on tips. No impetuous purchases after reading the business section of the newspaper (today that would include after watching business-talk television shows). No intuition plays. Do your homework. Get a grip on your objectivity. While it is possible for investors to learn from one another and share knowledge, be careful from whom you try to learn. Following the crowd can lead to nothing more than average (and too often less than average) return on invested capital. After all, the very definition of the word *average* is a characteristic describing the majority.

Graham's lesson apparently was easy enough for Bill Miller to comprehend. An independent thinker himself, fresh, original, brash, and daring—sometimes confoundingly intellectual and occasionally wrong—Miller was drawn to Graham's free-spirited approach to investment analysis. Miller in turn encourages his employees to engage in "thought experiments," and a fair number of his ideas are based on the cutting edge where natural sciences and economics get spliced together.

ECONOMICS UNDER A MICROSCOPE

When he sets out to inspire his fund managers, Miller is known to concoct an analogy between insects and stock pickers. Both, he says, must learn to efficiently identify "large but rare" finds and "small but common" ones. "Everything," he says, "potentially has investment implications."[1]

When Miller decided to put money behind AOL in late 1996, he drew on another image borrowed from science—a pile of buttons and strands of thread—an analogy he heard from theoretical biologist Stuart Kauffman. At that time, AOL was swamped by a rolling wave of business, and some experts thought that buyers frustrated by poor service would walk away en masse from their subscriptions. But Miller thought that like buttons linked by strands of thread, a critical mass of computer users already had AOL connections and would feel tied to the service. They would stick it out.

"All AOL is is connections," said Miller. Since AOL had already captured 40 percent of the market, Miller figured it would be tough for a competitor to knock the on-line service out of the lead.[2]

In Robert Hagstrom's book *Latticework: The New Investing*, he explains that despite Miller's independence, he advanced his investment knowledge with the help of others. But he separated himself from the grazing herd by extending his education beyond the standard curriculum of the investment world, with its litany of guidelines and measurements. "It is not even accurate to say that he peeked over the fence at other disciplines," wrote Hagstrom. "With energy and passion he *charged* over those fences, engaging himself in a careful study of physics, biology, philosophy, and psychology. He then worked to connect the lessons he learned in other disciplines back to the investment world."[3]

PRAGMATISM AS THE BACKDROP

It was as a graduate student in philosophy at Johns Hopkins that Miller began to understand himself as a pragmatist. In many ways this came as a natural result of a Johns Hopkins education, since some of the most notable pragmatists in American history—nineteenth-century education reformer John Dewey and philosopher William James—were associated with the Baltimore school.

Peter Lynch in his book *One Up on Wall Street* advises investors to use the tools they have. If you work at a water company and perhaps are an expert on that industry, concentrate on water utility stocks. If you are involved in the medical field, use what you know about medical products and services to spot investment opportunities. Miller does something similar. He approaches investing as a philosopher because that is his background. As a student of philosophy, he thinks in terms of evidence and what it reveals about a subject.

According to philosophers, explains Miller, there are three basic theories of truth, the correspondence theory, the coherence theory, and the pragmatic theory. People who adhere to the correspondence theory adopt a deep concept about how the world is structured and try to fit the world into the model. Because this model often is flawed or too rigid, this approach doesn't work well for investors. The coherence theory explains truth in terms of its coherence with an entire body of claims or beliefs. Again, applying the coherence theory to investments is a fuzzy way of approaching the markets. Miller is a pragmatist because "Pragmatic theorists use the test of usefulness and utility, not the test of correspondence."[4]

As a pragmatist, Miller has no infatuation with absolute standards, but rather turns his attention to results. He prefers to base both his ideas and actions on those processes that actually work—whatever it is that helps people achieve their goals.

Wearing the colors of a pragmatist has helped Miller remain mentally flexible and resilient. Whether considering the random walk theory, modern portfolio theory, or any other approach to investing, he has observed that models have a tendency to work for a while. Then suddenly, for no obvious reason, they stop working. All too often investors who have committed themselves to a theory stubbornly stick with it, even when the evidence screams that something is amiss. What this amounts to, Miller observes, is an adherence to absolute principles.

"If you have a correspondence theory of truth," he says, "you normally will hold on to that model for a whole lot longer because you believe it captures some deep structure in the markets, something that corresponds, in other words, to real things leading to outperformance."[5]

A pragmatist has an easier time letting go of shopworn ideas than most people do. "If you have a pragmatic theory," says Miller, "you typically have a shorter trigger to jettison the whole model, but more importantly you will realize that the model is there only to help you do a certain task."[6]

While pragmatism seems a simple enough notion, it isn't to be confused with the mundane or the ordinary. The ideas Miller ponders and attempts to apply to investment problems are anything but mundane. He draws his concepts from free-ranging sources, the foremost among them being the high-minded, high-altitude Santa Fe Institute. Perched at more than 7,000 feet on a sunny hill overlooking historic Santa Fe, the nonprofit, multidisciplinary think tank devotes much of its resources to the exploration of complex adaptive systems. Suffice it to say that Miller can go to Santa Fe to toy with abstract ideas. "Bill comes here and absorbs some of the scientific ideas and uses them to test his own way of thinking," explains Brian Arthur.[7]

PHYSICS ENTERS THE PICTURE

In 1987, just after the stock market crash, Miller read an article by *New York Times* science writer James Gleick on chaos theory. The article both introduced Miller to the Santa Fe Institute and caused him to wonder if such work could have any relevance for investors. After all, the economy, like other complex systems studied at SFI, is a multiagent environment with many local rules and feedback loops. Lacking a simple cause-and-effect model, it is impossible to predict what next month's or next year's market will be. Longer time predictions are even more out of the question. Admittedly, the chaos theory recognizes that deep within the chaos, there is order. But the order may be too buried to find it and apply it practically.

Five years later, John Reed, then Citicorp chairman, encouraged Miller to check out the Santa Fe Institute, a virtual camp for rocket scientists. Many of the people associated with SFI also have connections to the nearby Los Alamos National Laboratory, the place where the atomic bomb was developed and high-level nuclear research continues. On a juniper-studded hill, in casual Southwest splendor, SFI scholars such as Murray Gellmann, the Nobel Prize–winning physicist, hold forth on such esoteric topics as chaos theory, swarm theory, and what happens in adaptive nonlinear networks such as the human nervous and immune systems, natural ecologies and economies.

During his stay at SFI, Miller got pulled into long and intense discourses between business leaders, economists and biologists, physicists and others involved in the natural science of complexity. The goal of these discussions was to encourage a cross-fertilization that might infuse economics with fresh ideas. It was the study of complex adaptive systems Miller encountered at the Santa Fe Institute that prompted him to think about buttons and thread, ant colonies and even alluvial geography.

One of the interesting things about Miller's investing style is that he moves back and forth between two economic theories: one of them neoclassic and well accepted (with its assumption of diminishing returns) and the other a more controversial new-economy concept (incorporating increasing returns or positive feedback).

Miller became grounded in the latter theory after talking to a member of the intellectual glitterati he met at SFI, the Irish-born Brian Arthur (mentioned in Chapter 1), a scientist-turned-economist who formerly taught at Stanford University. Arthur probably is best known to the public for supplying the theoretical expertise that Justice Department lawyers used in the antitrust case against Microsoft. While Arthur's ideas can be extravagantly abstract, as the following pages prove, many of his concepts lend themselves easily to practical applications. Arthur, thanks perhaps to the contentious Irish intellectual tradition, is a renegade who turns his back on the certainty that scientists are trained to seek.

■■■■   LOSS OF CERTAINTY

Whatever the basis of his thinking, Arthur spotted an important trend: "The story of the sciences of the 20th Century is one of a steady loss of certainty. Much of what was real and machine-like and objective and determinate at the start of the century, by mid-century was a phantom, unpredictable, subjective and indeterminate. What had defined science at the start of the century—its power to predict, its clear subject/object distinction—no longer defines it at the end. Science after science has lost its innocence. Science after science has grown up."[8]

Arthur jabs away at the commonly held belief that the economy is an object that can be viewed mechanistically. Quite to the contrary, he believes, "the economy itself emerges from our subjective beliefs. These subjective beliefs are a-priori or deductively indeterminate in advance. They co-evolve, arise, decay, change, mutually reinforce and mutually negate. Subject and object cannot be neatly separated. And so the economy shows behavior that we can best describe as organic, rather than mechanistic. It is not a well-ordered, gigantic machine. It is organic. At all levels, it contains pockets of indeterminacy. It emerges from subjectivity and falls back into subjectivity."[9] (More about all of this later in the chapter when the subject of mistaken assumptions arises.)

Arthur, who chooses to live in California's Silicon Valley because it is a hotbed of futuristic thinking, coached Miller in the developing science of complexity and of adaptive nonlinear networks. Nonlinear networks, by their very nature, Arthur explains, do not act merely in terms of stimulus and response. They also anticipate. In economic systems, for example, participants form expectations: They construct their own models of the economy and act on the basis of predictions generated by their models.[10] The very expectations of players make things happen.

The stock market behaves in exactly that way, Arthur explains, when it sets the price of stocks—or prices assets—on a moment-by-moment basis: "Agents—investors—act as market statisticians," he notes. "They continually generate expectational models—interpretations of what moves prices in the market—and test these by trading. They discard and replace models if not successful. Expectations in the market therefore become endogenous—they continually change and adapt to a market that they together create."[11]

Simply stated, people decide what they think the stock market will do, then act accordingly. If enough investors predict the same thing, they buy and sell in a way that moves the price of a particular stock. Taken in aggregate, they move the market's general direction up or down. When feelings are either neutral or equally split, a stock price or the market as a whole remains flat. Massachusetts Institute of Technology economist Paul Krugman has suggested that Adam Smith's "invisible hand" is exactly the same as the economy in its continually adaptive state. As actors in the economy try to satisfy their individual material needs, buying and selling with other actors, they together create a marketplace.

THE STOCK MARKET SWARM

And then there is the swarm theory. Ben Graham noted that in some mysterious and unexplainable way, mispriced stocks, whether they were overvalued or undervalued, eventually returned to intrinsic value. Based on this pattern, some economists say the stock market adheres to the swarm theory. It acts like a swarm of bees. Although each individual bee might appear to be buzzing around aimlessly, it is acting as part of its swarm. The swarm itself has intelligence. The swarm knows where the food is and how to get it back to the hive by the most efficient path.

"It is fascinating to see how complex intelligent behavior can emerge from simple rules and numerous interactions without any plan or centralized coordination. Algorithms inspired by social insects can be applied in many disciplines," states writer Bertrand Ducharme.[12]

Eric Bonabeau, one of the seminal researchers on swarm intelligence, explains, "Forget centralization and control; forget programming; forget the concept of a big, omniscient computer;

think of a hive or an anthill. Social insect colonies aren't centrally controlled; they're composed of thousands or even millions of insects with limited cognitive repertoires. Individually, one insect can't do much, but collectively social insects can achieve great things—build a nest, forage for food, take care of the brood, allocate labor, and so on. The collective intelligence of social insects, swarm intelligence, offers a powerful new tool for computing."[13]

"At a time when the world is growing so complex," he continues, "no single human being can understand it—when information, and not the lack of it, threatens our lives; when users can no longer master bloated software, swarm intelligence offers an alternative way of designing computing systems. In swarms, autonomy emergency and distributed functioning replace control, preprogramming, and centralization."[14]

With swarm intelligence, as with the stock market, the best ideas get reinforced and others evaporate.

More about bugs. When termites initiate nest construction, a certain sequence of events occurs, explains Danish molecular biologist Jesper Hoffmeyer. "First, hundreds of termites move around at random, while they exhibit a peculiar habit of dropping small pellets of masticated earth in places which are elevated a little bit from the ground. In spite of the disorganized character of this activity, it results in the formation of small heaps of salivated earth pellets. Second, these heaps of earth pellets are interpreted by the termites as a sign to release a new habit. Every time a termite meets a heap it energetically starts building earth pellets on top of it. The effect of this activity will soon be the formation of a vertical column. The activity stops when the column has reached a certain species-specific height. Third, if the column has no immediate neighbors the termites completely stop bothering about it. But if in an adequate distance there are one or more other columns, a third habit is released. The termites climb the columns and start building in a sloping direction towards the neighboring column. In this way the columns become connected with arches."[15]

A CONCEPT WITH PRACTICAL APPLICATIONS

During their conversations, Arthur talked to Miller about an evolving economic principle dear to his heart called increasing returns, which are a sort of positive feedback: the tendency of anything that's ahead to get farther ahead, or if falling behind, to get farther behind. This is the twin, or perhaps the reverse image, of the classic economic concept of diminishing returns.

Economists, claims Arthur, have sniffed around the theory of increasing returns for 100 years or so. Such towering economic thinkers as Alfred Marshall asked the question: Instead of returns that diminish as an economic unit expands and matures, what if businesses gained an advantage as they took on larger and larger markets? But for the longest time, the possibility of increasing returns seemed easy to discount. Arthur recalls that when he was a graduate student in economics in the 1970s, the distaste for increasing returns was at its crest: "All results in economics were served to us with the incantation that they were true," wrote Arthur, "providing there is sufficient convexity—that is, diminishing returns on the margin. I was curious about what might happen when there were increasing returns on the margin, but none of my professors seemed interested in the question or willing to answer it."[16]

But the notion continued to intrigue Arthur and eventually he began to see a link between increasing returns and the economics of technology. "The standard technology problem in economics was that of figuring out the economic circumstances under which a new, superior technology might replace an old inferior one, and how long this process might take. But from my engineering studies as an undergraduate (Arthur was an undergraduate at Queens University in Belfast, Northern Ireland, and pursued his graduate studies at the University of California, Berkeley), I was aware that a new technology normally came along in several different versions or design formats. Thus if a new technology were to replace an old one these alternatives might well be thought of as in competition for adopters. Further, it seemed this learning effect would provide advantage to any version that got ahead in cumulative adoptions; and so the adoption process could lock in, by historical chance, to whichever version of the technology got a better start. It was clear that this 'competing-technologies problem' was par excellence one of increasing returns and it seemed just right for the approach I was trying to develop."[17]

The idea that economies could be based on increasing returns continued to be regarded with skepticism by most economists as recently as the mid-1980s. When the paradigm shift occurred, however, it came quickly, and increasing returns now are considered central to international trade theory, the economics of technology, industrial organization, macroeconomics, regional economics, growth theory, economic development, and political economy.

PARALLEL WORLDS

Today, diminishing returns and increasing returns are recognized as operating side-by-side. In that part of the economy to which diminishing returns apply, there are many companies, and they tend to share markets. As one company grows large, it runs into more and more difficulties. Arthur says, "So you get bound into an equilibrium and a high degree of stability in markets and nothing much happens. In these markets, you don't hear that Bill Gates has just bought a steel company and that company is about to take over all of the steel in the United States. . . . Or that somebody's started a lumber company and in five years there is an IPO and that person is now worth half a billion dollars. This is not like Netscape."[18]

In a climate of diminishing returns, writes Arthur, "Economic actions eventually engender a negative feedback that leads to a predictable equilibrium for prices and market share. Negative feedback tends to stabilize the economy because any major changes will be offset by the very reactions they generate. The high oil prices of the 1970s encouraged energy conservation and increased oil exploration, precipitating a predictable drop in the prices (in the 1980s). According to conventional theory the equilibrium marks the 'best' outcome possible under the circumstance: The most efficient use and allocation of resources."[19]

INCREASING OR DIMINISHING RETURNS?

"In the market of diminishing returns, the more you get ahead, by increasing your market share or your market, the sooner you run into difficulties, with increased costs or lower profits," says Arthur.[20] For example, the larger a petroleum company becomes, the farther away it must go in search of oil fields, and the higher exploration and shipping costs become. The same holds true for mining companies.

Those parts of the economy that are resource based, such as agriculture, bulk-goods production, the timber industry, and so forth, are still for the most part subject to diminishing returns. Conventional economics dominate. In the knowledge-based economy, increasing returns hold sway. Products such as computers, pharmaceuticals, missiles, aircraft, automobiles, software, telecommunications equipment, and fiber optics are complicated to design and manufacture, requiring large initial investments in research, development, and tooling. But once sales begin, incremental production is relatively cheap. A new airframe or aircraft engine, for example, typically costs between $2 billion and $3 billion to design, develop, certify, and put into production. Yet each subsequent copy costs around $50 million to $100 million. Unit costs fall and profits increase as more units are built.[21]

"The evolution of the VCR market would not have surprised the great Victorian economist Alfred Marshall, one of the founders of today's conventional economics," says Arthur. "In his 1890 *Principles of Economics* he noted that if firms' production costs fall as their market share increases, a firm that by good fortune gained a high proportion of the market early on would be able to best its rivals; 'whichever firm first gets off to a good start' would corner the market. Marshall did not follow up on this observation, however, and theoretical economics in this century has until recently largely ignored it."[22]

As the market for showing movies at home using videotape evolved, there was competition between Beta and VHS video recorders. Beta is considered the superior product and the one most often used by professionals. Yet VHS got ahead in sales and became dominant, at least for a while. Now both Beta and VHS technology are being replaced by DVD technology.

While it may be distressing that second-rate technologies some-times prevail, it's not all bad. Arthur says the fact that returns can be increasing is good news. "Diminishing returns made [philosopher Thomas] Carlyle call economics a dismal science. Increasing returns maybe makes economics a cheerful science."[23]

Some companies operate in an environment of both increasing and decreasing returns—for example, IBM and Hewlett-Packard. Both are involved in high-tech development and in the manufacture of old economy–type products and equipment. While IBM produces software, networking systems, and other new economy products, its computers are similar to an old-economy commodity. In HP's case, many of the company's plotters, scanners, and other products are hy-brids of new and old economy products. They are partly based on software development (more likely to be subject to increasing re-turns) and partly on hardware (more likely to operate in the realm of decreasing returns).

In the high-tech environment, several conditions exist that tip the scales from diminishing to increasing returns. These three traits—cost advantage, network effects, and groove-in—can lead to lock-in.

COST ADVANTAGE

New technology products are different from low-tech ones because they are incredibly complicated. They have high up-front costs, but are inexpensive to replicate.

A case in point: Microsoft Windows was mightily costly to de-sign. The program required high levels of expertise and lots of time, which ran up research and development costs. With Windows 95, the first disk cost approximately $250 million. But the second and all subsequent disks cost just a few cents. The more disks that are burned during the life of the product, the lower the per-unit cost. Therefore, the larger Microsoft Windows' market gets, the more cost advantage accrues to Microsoft, and the more Bill Gates gets a head-lock on the title of richest man on the planet.

Not only does the unit cost shrink, but increased production brings other benefits. More units out the door means the company is gaining more experience in the manufacturing process and greater understanding of how to make each subsequent unit even cheaper. Moreover, experience gained with one product or technology can smooth the path for new products that incorporate similar or related technologies. Japan, for example, leveraged an initial investment in precision instruments into the ability to manufacture all sorts of consumer electronics products. From there the Japanese progressed to the integrated circuits required for the electronic devices themselves.[24]

Something interesting, and formerly unexpected, happens in a market with increasing returns. According to Arthur, "When two or more increasing return technologies 'compete' then, for a 'market' of potential adopters, insignificant events may by chance give one of them an initial advantage in adoptions. This technology may then improve more than the others may, so it may appeal to a wider proportion of potential adopters. It may therefore become further adopted and further improved. Thus it may happen that a technology that by chance gains an early lead in adoption may eventually 'corner the market' of potential adopters, with other technologies becoming locked out."[25]

THE FIRST-TO-GET-OUT ADVANTAGE

There are plenty of examples in the corporate world of businesses losing an advantageous position because management didn't fully understand the mechanisms of the market—IBM and Apple Computer, both of which suffered at the hands of Microsoft, are two of the best known.

There also are many cases of technologies, not always the best ones, locked in by "founder effects." The early advantage effects occur for the smallest reason—a key player of a competitor calling in sick for a week, a minor government regulation, a bad storm that closed or slowed business for a brief time. The fact that small events, accidents, coincidences, and so forth have a major impact on the outcome is called sensitive dependence on initial conditions. According to some experts, John Montgomery, a Californian experimenting with flight, lost out to the Wright Brothers because of the San Francisco earthquake of 1906. The QWERTY typewriter keyboard, alternating current versus direct current in electrical systems, and nuclear reactor technology in the 1950s and 1960s represent other examples of the wide adoption of less-than-optimal technologies. In the last case, the light-water reactor dominates the market because it was chosen to power nuclear submarines and took precedence over gas-cooled reactors.

Although there are risks surrounding the time and money used to develop new products, the early advantage can lead to network effects. Before a product is locked in, however, it must go through the network effect and groove-in stage.

NETWORK EFFECTS

Network effects kick in because the more people who use a product, the more others feel compelled to use it, or are forced to use it because of its popularity. The bigger a network gets, the more likely a consumer feels pressure to join the network. Take another Microsoft product—its Word for Windows word processing program. Many who use word processing claim that WordPerfect is a superior program, that it is easier to use. Yet because Word is packaged with Windows and comes free with so many computers, it is more commonly used. Because so many businesses and individuals utilize Word, their customers and suppliers are compelled to have it as well. The network effect leads to positive feedback in which the product's presence in the market increases.

Perhaps the most familiar example of the importance of networking was the development of the telephone. When very few people had a telephone, the instrument wasn't of much use; but when a larger number of people had a telephone (or a computer with access to e-mail), it became enormously useful. When almost everyone has a product, it becomes essential.

GROOVE-IN

Groove-in is often discussed as an element on its own, but it primarily represents the next stage of network effects. The tendency for a consumer to select a product is amplified as more accessories such as software are developed around it. The product is said to "groove in." The more Microsoft Word is loaded onto computers as a freebie, the more people become familiar with it. The more Word-compatible software they buy, the more they need to upgrade to the latest version, and around it goes. Such has been the case with Java, the downloading language for the Internet. The more it is used, the more everyone needs to have it loaded onto their computers. The stage is set for lock-in.

LOCK-IN

Perhaps the most familiar example of "lock-in" occurs in presidential primaries. A candidate may not be the best candidate, but if he (or she) gets and holds a lead, he can attract more to campaign coffers, get the lion's share of media coverage, attract a following who expects him to win, and soon lock in a victory.

"You get these dominances," explains Arthur. "In high tech, you see companies getting very wealthy, cash rich, buying other companies, merging, and so on. You don't see this in steel and lumber and cement and dog chow and corn flakes. There may be large branded companies, but you don't see anything quite like high tech."[26]

For years, business schools taught that it was not smart to be the first into the market. Let others enter first and make all the mistakes, then learn from them as a late starter. This assumption went hand-in-hand with another: that in a free market, the superior technology will triumph. These two principles often do work in situations of constant or diminishing returns. Yet in the world of high technology, an early-start technology may capture the market in such a way that a new and potentially superior late arrival cannot gain a footing. The best product doesn't always win out.[27]

"This notion that the market is always wonderful and perfect," says Arthur, "is a right-wing ideological idea. People don't expect that all the friends they have are the most optimal friends. People get married; sometimes it's wonderful and sometimes it isn't. Lock-ins occur; sometimes for the best, sometimes not."[28]

Fortunately for both consumers and competitors, lock-ins tend to last only about 10 years or so, until an entirely new technology takes over. In fact, in an atmosphere of increasing returns, there is a fairly predictable pattern.

STANDING ON SHAKY GROUND

Arthur explains, "There tends to be an instability when a market is just starting out, say Java versus ActiveX. It's often difficult to say how things are going to go. But as one side gets farther ahead, gets more advantage and locks in the market, there is a period of stability. Then nothing much happens until the next wave of technology rolls over into something for a while. Digital locks into mini-computers for 10 years. But then Digital is surpassed with workstations and PCs. That's one reason I'm not too concerned about lock-ins."[29]

The difficulty for investors in the new economy, he notes, is that there is a great deal of inherent instability and uncertainty, especially early in the product cycle. "In situations involving competition among objects whose 'market success' was cumulative or self-reinforcing," says Arthur, "I discovered that whenever I found such problems, they tended to have similar properties. There was typically more than one long-run equilibrium outcome. The one arrived at was not predictable in advance; it tended to get locked in; it was not necessarily the most efficient; and its 'selection' tended to be subject to historical events. If the problem was symmetrical in formulation, the outcome was typically asymmetrical."[30]

As a result, business strategy has to reach far beyond the usual premises relating to keeping costs down and quality up, developing core competency, and so forth. A new layer of complication is added in a game in which the winner can capture huge parts of the market and losers are left with almost nothing, even if their products are technically brilliant. "So basically the strategies are very much the strategies you would apply in presidential primaries. You want to build up market share. You want to built up user base. If you do, you can lock in that market," Arthur explains.[31]

It was with this goal in mind that Sun Microsystems gave away Java for free. Sun also formed a consortium to put up $100 million for software development to write applications in that language. The result was a momentum that became unstoppable. A similar thing happened with America Online, Prodigy, and Compuserve. Prodigy was first in the field, but America Online came along and gave away the browser. It wasn't clear which was the best service, but AOL prevailed and eventually bought Compuserve, becoming the dominant player.

PROBLEMS HAVE NO SOLUTIONS— GET USED TO IT

In the old-style economy, people believed that there were problems and there were solutions. In the high-tech, rising-return environment, attention turns to the dynamics, which are dominated by process rather than permanent results. Nothing is permanently settled or solved. Companies, managers and entrepreneurs all just keep moving, changing, adjusting, and adapting. Those old standbys— logical analysis and game theory—seldom apply. Given the number of unknowns and variables, it has become impossible to figure out the new economy in the old cognitive way.

ON THE OTHER HAND . . .

Not everyone agrees that the new economy operates any differently from the old one. Some economists have had difficulty accepting the pubescent concept of increasing returns, mainly because the principles call for multiple equilibria and outcomes that are almost impossible to predict.

The critics claim that the path-dependence school has yet to produce the "smoking gun" evidence it needs to show that the marketplace locks in to clearly inferior technology.[32] They insist that *lock-in* is just another word for *standardization*, which is good for industries and the societies in which standardization occurs. It's always easier to have just one kind of lightbulb outlet, drive on the same side of the road as everyone else, and use a standard array of batteries.

U of C Berkeley's Hal R. Varian is one of the world's most influential theorists on the network economy. He discounts any shift in economic theory. Rather he points out that computers and data networks have provided a higher level of information than ever before—even creating the "information economy." But, he asserts, "information has always been a notoriously difficult commodity to deal with, and in some ways, computers and high-speed networks make the problems of buying, selling, and distributing information goods worse rather than better."[33] Nevertheless, Varian argues, Internet commerce must adhere to established economic rules.

"Ignore basic economic principles at your own risk. Technology changes. Economic laws do not," he writes.[34]

Furthermore, Arthur also has been set upon by packs of Libertarians who accuse him of heretical statements—that is, that free markets don't work. "I never said that," Arthur declares. "I am a great admirer of markets."[35] Despite his fondness for free markets, he thinks people need to be less naive.

"The Libertarians are upset," says Arthur, "because I'm saying that the invisible hand is not perfect. Indeed, the invisible hand is a little bit arthritic. It's pretty good, but it's slightly less than perfect. I think we need to grow up and recognize this."[36] It shouldn't be disappointing that lock-in occurs and sometimes inferior products win, especially to those who realize economics isn't like religion, to be believed with blind faith. It is a science, to be studied and understood, and to be continually questioned.

Arthur emphasizes that he would like to see economics, a 200-year-old discipline, become more of a science, and that would mean concerning itself more with reality. Nevertheless, Miller wrote, "Our portfolio doesn't depend on our being right at the twists and turns of the economy. It depends on our understanding the prospects for our companies and what is discounted in their share prices."[37]

THE DANGER OF MISTAKEN ASSUMPTIONS

As if he hadn't shaken up traditionalists enough, Arthur preaches that there is great danger that economic theory (or any scientific precept) could be built on rigorous deductions that themselves are based on faulty assumptions. This has happened in other sciences from time to time, and when it does, the science finds itself in a state of disarray. In his 1954 book *Nature and the Greeks*, physicist Erwin Schrodinger writes, "The mistakes of the great, promulgated along with the discoveries of their genius, are apt to work havoc."[38]

In other words, garbage in, garbage out, and it is easy to delude people about garbage. "Somebody comes along and does beautiful work," says Arthur, "but the assumptions aren't quite right. Then that beautiful work becomes the gospel. There are arguments over the deduction but few are looking at the assumption."[39]

Arthur insists that economics has become hide-bound to an outdated framework. "For my money, the economists got away from really questioning at a deep level how the world works, how decisions actually got made," he explains. "If something doesn't conform to 'models,' it is deemed to be 'behavioral,' meaning that it is ad hoc, that people are somehow not behaving themselves properly. It's like seeing real economic behavior as impurities in a physical system or chemical system that are messing things up."[40]

The disconnection, says Arthur, has to do with what philosopher William Barrett called the illusion of technique, which in turn is related to a form of modernism that developed early in the twentieth century called logical positivism. It is based on the notion that you can take any scientific subject—say philosophy, logic, linguistics, mathematics, physics, or economics—and reduce it to a set of axioms, then deduce what you need to know from the axioms. "In other words," says Arthur, "build up the rest of the structure from a logical foundation. It's a wonderful idea but . . . it's totally cockeyed. It never really works. It hasn't worked in any field, including physics."[41]

THEORY IS NOT REAL LIFE

Arthur believes that the sort of rationality that has been assumed in economics—perfect, logical, deductive rationality—may be useful in solving theoretical problems, but usually does not work in a real-life scenario. Deductive rationality, he maintains, "demands much of human behavior—much more in fact than it can usually deliver." As a system, it breaks down in complex situations for two main reasons: First, beyond a certain level of complexity, our logical mind ceases to cope. There is simply too much to know and analyze. Take a game of checkers, versus a more complicated game, for example. It may be easy to follow rational reasoning to win a checkers game, but in chess, bridge, or backgammon, it becomes more difficult. As the complications grow, the very problem becomes more difficult to define. Second, just as we can't be fully rational in complex situations, we can't rely on other players to be rational. We are forced to guess their behavior. Shared assumptions cease to apply. As a result, humans quite naturally turn to inductive reasoning.

Inductive reasoning leads us in the right direction because, explains Arthur, "we are superb at seeing or recognizing or matching patterns—behaviors that confer obvious and evolutionary benefits. In complicated problems we seek patterns, then simplify the problem by using the pattern as a model."

Economists have been reluctant to adopt inductive reasoning as a scientific method, although Arthur says simple models "enable us to deal with ill-definedness. Where we have insufficient definition, our working models fill the gap."[43]

"NOBODY GOES THERE ANYMORE. IT'S TOO CROWDED"—YOGI BERRA

To further illustrate the pitfalls of mistaken assumptions, Arthur constructed what he calls the Bar Problem, or the El Farol example. In this example, Arthur tries to anticipate how many people will show up on Thursday nights at the funky Santa Fe watering hole, El Farol, to hear Irish music. If a person went to the bar on an earlier occasion and it was too crowded for comfort, he is unlikely to return immediately. But if on the night he first attended the bar it was at the ideal capacity, he and the other customers are likely to return. This leads to a tendency toward overcrowding until people stop coming and attendance declines to a point where the conditions are more ideal, or even to the point that there are too few customers. This "dynamic of numbers" can apply to various economic situations. Certainly it applied to AOL, as the Internet access provider added customers faster than it added customer service, although in time AOL was able to meet the demand.[44]

Miller also addresses the issue of mistaken assumptions, relating it to his securities analysis technique. He cautions investors to be on their guard.

> "*Too many people*," Miller says, "*underperform because they have a money management style that makes no sense. Namely, they try to forecast variables that are unforecastable. Nobody can forecast interest rates or GDP [gross domestic product] numbers. People who base their portfolio on forecasts are basing it on something that is inherently subject to large error.*"[45]

More information about Miller's ways of avoiding this type of error is in Chapter 3. In that chapter we will also learn about investors from the past who have influenced Miller's thinking.

ECONOMICS—SANTA FE STYLE

The visionary scientists at the Santa Fe Institute came up with four characteristics of the economy that today's investors would do well to heed:

1. *Interaction is dispersed.* When something happens in the economy, it's based on the interaction of numerous individual agents, all acting at the same time. Individual agents anticipate the actions of other agents and base their own decisions on the anticipated actions of others.

2. *There is no global controller of the economy.* Although it is true that there are laws and governing institutions at multiple levels, no single entity does, or is capable of, controlling the overall economy. Instead, the competition and cooperation between agents provide the control.

3. *The economy continually adapts to new conditions.* The economy is in continual motion with new strategies, actions, results of behavior, products, services, and players. In a continuing dynamism, the agents change their own behavior in response to new things, which in turn forces other agents to adapt.

4. *The economy seldom, if ever, achieves equilibrium.* Classical economists believed that when change occurred, the economy automatically sought equilibrium. Because of the ever-changing character of the economy, equilibrium is now seen as merely an ideal but abstract situation.[46]

CHAPTER 3

THE ART OF VALUATION

When you come to a fork in the road, take it.

Yogi Berra

Bill Miller was a spunky 9-year-old, mowing lawns for spending money, when he accidentally discovered the stock market. He came in from a sweaty job in the Florida sun, for which he was paid not more than $1. "My father was reading something that looked different from the sports pages or the comics. I asked what he was reading," Miller recalled. His father, who was a baseball coach for a while but for most of his life worked as a manager at a trucking company and in sales, was reading the financial pages. He pointed to a column in the stock tables with a +1/4th in it. "He said, 'If you'd owned a share of this company yesterday, you'd have 25 cents more today than you had yesterday.' I said, 'How do you make that happen?' " Miller's father replied that you didn't do anything to make it happen. It happened by itself.

"That sounded pretty easy to me," Miller said, in contrast to the toil he had just endured to earn a buck. His interest was further piqued when in high school he read his first investment book, *How I Made $2 Million in the Stock Market,* a book written by a dancer who became a specialist in reading stock charts. Miller bought his first shares when he was 16, using $75 he earned as a baseball umpire. He invested the $75 in RCA and made about $600 in profits, which he immediately squandered on a second-hand Triumph TR4 convertible. Later, when he began earning his living by delivering higher returns after fees and taxes than an investor could earn on an index fund, he woke up to a new reality. "I've since learned it is easy to make the market return, but you can do lots and lots of work and you still may not be able to beat the market averages."

▬▬ MAKING THE VALUE CONNECTION

Some years after his lawn-mowing days, Miller became an undergraduate majoring in economics at Washington and Lee University. There he was introduced to value investing and the thinking of Benjamin Graham. "Once someone explains the value concept to you, either you get it or you don't," he said. Miller got it. "I found the concept to be congenial. It made sense." Later on down the road, Miller became acquainted with the writings of John Burr Williams, which provided another layer of analysis atop the value base. But basically, he remained attracted to the value philosophy because it required rigorous thinking and disciplined executions, although he eventually put his own liberal spin on Graham.

**How to Calculate Future Value,
Present Value, or Rate of Return of a Business**

Calculating discounting to present value is made easier by using the Texas Instruments financial, solar-powered calculator, the BA-35. Given the expected return on an investment, the number of years the investment is held, and the present value, it is possible to calculate the future value of that investment. Alternatively, given the desired future value, you can calculate the present value, or given the present and future values, the required rate of return can be calculated.

(Continued)

The calculator keys involved are: *PV* (present value), *FV* (future value), *N* (number of years investment held), % *i* (rate of return), and *CPT* (compute).

Using an example where the present value of an investment is $1,000, the rate of return is 8%, and the investment is held for 10 years, you can calculate the future value of the investment as follows: Enter $1,000 = *PV*, 10 = *N*, and 8 = % *i*, press *CPT* followed by *FV*, and the calculator will show the future value as $2,159.

Alternatively, using the future value to find the present value: Enter $2,159 = *FV*, 8 = % *i*, 10 = *N*, press *CPT* followed by *PV*, and the calculator will show the present value as $1,000.

John Burr Williams' formula:

$$V_0 = \sum_{t=1}^{t=\infty} \pi_t v^t = \pi_1 v + \pi_2 v^2 + \pi_3 v^3 + \cdots \qquad (1a)$$

where :

V_0 = investment value at start

π_t = dividend in year t

$$v = \frac{1}{1+i}, \text{ by definition} \qquad (2)$$

i = interest rate sought by the investor

For bonds :

$$V_0 = \sum_{t=1}^{t=n} \pi_t v^t + Cv^n \qquad (1b)$$

where :

π_t = coupon in year t

C = face value, or principal, of bond

n = number of years to maturity

BENJAMIN GRAHAM—
THE ORIGINAL INTELLIGENT INVESTOR

Benjamin Graham, who died in 1976, was a cool-headed academic who, like Miller, was a student of philosophy, math, and science. Graham ran the Wall Street investment firm of Graham Newman Inc. For decades, Graham taught a graduate-level course at Columbia University, where he coached many of the most important investors of the twentieth century, including Warren Buffett. In his spare time, Graham wrote books that sell nearly as well today as they did when they were first published more than 50 years ago. Thanks to his classic works *Security Analysis* and *The Intelligent Investor,* Graham is considered by most financial historians to be the father of value investing. Most people think of Graham as someone who tried to buy stocks at below the company's asset value, so if the company went broke, he could at least get his money back once the company's tangible assets were sold. Indeed, Graham did a lot of that type of investing in the decades after the Crash of 1929 when there was an enormous number of distressed stocks available. But there was a lot more to Graham's investment style than buying cheap so that an investor had a wide margin of safety.

Those who probe deeper into his work soon learn that Graham's fundamental contribution to the investment world was that he brought the clarity of logic and reason to the investment process. When he started out on Wall Street in 1914, Graham realized that investment decisions generally were made either under the spell of salesmanship or in moods of excessive optimism or pessimism. Graham rose above his peers by gathering facts, thinking objectively, and conducting sound analysis. The price is what you *pay* for an asset, he would say, but value is what you *get*.

Graham believed that all stocks have an intrinsic or basic value, and although a stock may trade above or below its actual value, the price invariably will revert to intrinsic value at some point. Just as a buyer might try to get the best price on a car or a home so that he can make a profit (or at least avoid getting scorched) when he later sells, Graham strove to identify bargain securities. To recognize a low-priced stock or bond, an investor must be able to calculate (if only approximately) its intrinsic value. Graham taught his disciples to ignore both the price cycles of individual stocks and movements of the market as a whole. These gyrations were of little consequence to Graham, except that they provided opportunities to buy low and sell high. Downturns provided bargains by the basketful and bull markets brought on the buyers willing to pay top prices.

By tradition and training, value investors have pored over income statements, balance sheets, and other historical documents searching for clues to the true worth of a company. Although Graham looked at a company as a whole and considered its future earnings potential, ultimately he placed the greatest emphasis on debt levels, tangible asset value, and backward-looking indicators such as price-to-earnings ratios. He was suspicious of future earnings estimates, especially those made by management, because they were so speculative and so often proved incorrect.

All this exactitude had great appeal to Miller, who addresses investing from the value perspective, but is not dogmatic about the value tradition. Investing, he says, involves digging through all kinds of information and attempting to figure out which company has the highest probability of increasing in price over the long term. To paraphrase Ben Graham, even a dog-stock is a bargain at the right price.

"Estimates of business value," Miller notes, "are subject to substantial uncertainty arising from, but not limited to, the availability of accurate information, economic growth, changes in competitive conditions, technological change, changes in government policy or geopolitical dynamics, and so forth. We attempt to minimize the potentially unfavorable

consequences of errors in the estimation of business value by building in a margin of safety between our estimates and the price we are willing to pay for a security."[1]

Miller says he uses a variety of both quantitative and qualitative methods to achieve this end. The quantitative work includes, but is not limited to

- Tools of traditional valuation such as price-to-earnings, price–to–book value, and price–to–cash flow ratios, both future looking, and historic
- Extensive comparative valuation work including historic, future looking, and scenario-based methods
- Volatility, but only to the extent that volatility allows him to buy low and sell high
- Discounted cash flow and free cash flow analyses
- Private market and liquidation value analysis

The qualitative assessment measures include but are not limited to

- Studying companies' products, competitive positioning, and strategy
- Analyzing industry economics and dynamics
- Evaluating regulatory frameworks

Although the spreadsheets used by Miller and his associates to do the necessary calculations vary in size, they are typically 7 pages long with 350 lines on a page, with data 15 columns across. "Because we have concentrated portfolios and frequently take large stakes in companies," explains Mark Niemann, "we need a high level of confidence. We build valuation models that represent the underlying economic reality."[2]

OPENING THE WINDOW
FOR A BROADER VIEW

Miller was among those investors who realized that in the new millennium high-tech economy, Graham's teachings might not be entirely efficient. "Value investors have ended up in tangible-asset businesses, mainly manufacturing and natural resources companies," said Miller. "But those companies are an ever-smaller part of the economy and the market. If you limit yourself in that way, you're going to miss opportunities."[3]

Additionally, Graham's methods tended to be static in nature and didn't always make a smooth transition into a knowledge-based revolutionary and dynamic economy.

Miller understands that sometimes evaluation problems arise from outside influences. Wherever the confusion comes from, it shows that investors need to understand that the bottom line can change, depending on how the numbers are arranged. In the early 1990s, for example, some companies were told they had to put their postretirement health care benefits on the balance sheet and take a charge for them. General Motors' book value went from $55 to $5. "What's the sense of price-to-book when one day it's $55 and the next day it's $5?" asked Miller. "The company hasn't changed, only the accounting metrics. We adjust the accounting metrics for the underlying economic reality."[4]

Despite the drawbacks and limitations, Miller believes that traditional value investing still has merit. "You just can't use overly simplified valuation techniques to substitute for analysis and thinking," he warns.[5] And remember, he continues, "we use [valuation] metrics as landmarks and not roadblocks. You don't want to have a static approach in a dynamic world."[6]

▮▮▮▮   LOOKING BACKWARD

When Miller looks at Graham's favorite numbers, he puts a lesser weighting on them than other value managers might. Before using historical figures, Miller explains, investors should ask how much relevance the past will have on future earnings and profits. "If you have a company like U.S. Steel, and you picked it in 1903 when it was founded, you would see that it had many prosperous years. But it has always been in slow decline. A trader might buy it [on a day when the price was down], but to buy it, an investor must feel it was overly discounted, or would have to feel that some fundamental had changed."[7]

"From a theoretical view," he continues, "there are flaws using the backward looking stuff. At the end of the day, 100 percent of the value of any equity depends on the future, not on the past."[8]

Therefore, Miller sometimes buys stocks with a high price in relation to earnings, which in the past would have been anathema to a value investor. Just because a particular company has a high P/E ratio, Miller claims, doesn't mean that it has not been severely mispriced in the market.

Besides being backward-looking, Miller says, "P/E ratios by themselves are irrelevant. They capture one factor in a stock and often have little to do with underlying values. Let me explain my approach this way. Somebody said to me six months ago (October, 1999), how could I own Dell Computer and not Gateway because Gateway is a much better value? I said, what do you mean? Well, he said, Gateway trades at 12 times earnings and Dell trades at 35 times earnings, so Gateway is obviously a better value. So I replied that I had two businesses for him

> *to invest in. In one he could earn a 200 percent return on his investment and in the other he could earn 40 percent. Which would he choose? Why, business number one of course, he said, it's five times as profitable. I said you just described the difference between Dell and Gateway. Dell earns 200 percent on its capital and Gateway 40 percent, yet Dell trades at only three times the P/E of Gateway."*[9]

Dell trades at a relatively high multiple because it earns a high return on capital, due to its sustainable competitive advantage as the low-cost leader in a commodity business. The company can constantly put pressure on competitors by lowering prices. Gateway has a similar advantage, but because it's smaller in terms of sales, it doesn't have the same leverage.

THOSE ELUSIVE EARNINGS FIGURES

Almost all investors, from the start of their education, are instructed to study earnings. There is no question that earnings can be a starting point, but some highly promising companies, especially young ones, have no earnings at all. Furthermore, earnings manipulation has been with us since the beginning of accounting time.

The latest wave of "creative accounting" began in the 1980s with the rise of earnings before interest, taxes, depreciation, and amortization (EBITDA), an early form of pro-forma reporting. In the 1990s, companies stretched EBITDA to new lengths, using aggressive tricks to show continually rising sales and earnings, and to drive share prices higher. When the market slumped in 2000 and afterwards, accounting contortions got worse.

While Generally Accepted Accounting Principles (GAAP) is the accounting standard required by the Securities and Exchange Commission, many companies—including many reputable ones—also present pro-forma figures, which tell their financial story in a way the company officers prefer. Some money managers (such as Miller) and CEOs (such as Warren Buffett) feel GAAP doesn't always present a true picture and that there is some merit in looking at an alternative presentation. The problem is, each company uses pro forma as it wishes, making it difficult to compare companies in the same or similar industries. It virtually takes an accountant to interpret pro-forma procedures to determine whether they are dependable or deceptive. This leads to concern in financial services about the validity of earnings reports.

For example, the giant telecommunications carrier, Qwest Communications International Inc., reported $2 billion in quarterly earnings before interest, taxes, depreciation, and amortization in a January 24, 2001, press release. Two weeks later, shareholders got their annual report and learned in a footnote that Qwest actually lost $116 million under GAAP accounting. Qwest claimed that the variation was extreme because of adjustments made for the takeover of U.S. West Inc.[10]

Some accountants call pro-forma results "EBS earnings"—Everything but Bad Stuff. At its worst, pro-forma accounting uses ploys to brighten a company's financial picture including

- Taking large and early write-offs in a year with poor earnings so that a subsequent recovery will look stronger
- Providing easy, generous financing to customers to boost sales, even if the customer has questionable credit capability
- Changing employee pension plans to lower operating costs, although sometimes this is a good thing to do
- Booking pending sales as if they'd already happened to make sales figures higher
- Failing to record future rebates or potential returns
- Promoting sales by granting big customers stock in the company or issuing cheap warrants

Of course, these methods make sales look stronger to stimulate the share price. The black magic is that they take a basically sound and defensible business practice and stretch it to the extreme. While professional analysts usually are able to see through these gambits, less experienced investors might very well swing at a bad pitch. Indeed, in May 2001, a *Business Week* editorial blasted pro-forma earnings as "deceptive, unwarranted, and down-right dangerous to the financial system."[11]

That same spring, at the urging of SEC Chief Accountant Lynn E. Turner, Financial Executives International, an organization of CFOs, issued guidelines intended to rein in the excesses in pro-forma accounting. The New York Society of Securities Analysts (NYSSA), which was founded by Benjamin Graham and his colleagues for just such purposes, organized a discussion group to focus attention on the way Amazon.com reports its results. Using Amazon as a convenient case study, NYSSA hoped to get companies to return to "reality-based" reporting.

JOHN BURR WILLIAMS

There are many ways to obfuscate earnings. Still, as John Burr Williams preached, earnings aren't the end-all, be-all of financial analysis. "Earnings," he notes, "are only a means to an end, and the means should not be mistaken for the end. Therefore we must say that a stock derives its value from its dividends, not its earnings. In short, a stock is worth only *what you can get out of it*. So, spoke the farmer to his son:

> A cow for her milk,
> A hen for her eggs,
> And a stock, by heck,
> For her dividends.

> An orchard for fruit,
> Bees for their honey,
> And stocks, besides,
> For their dividends.

"The old man knew where milk and honey came from but he made no such mistake as to tell his son to buy a cow for her cud or bees for their buzz," insisted Williams.[12]

Miller doesn't gather all of his ideas from futuristic economists such as Arthur. He has also been influenced by the more structured Williams, whose book, *The Theory of Investment Value*—highly original for its time—was first published by Harvard Press in 1938. It is no wonder an intellectualizer such as Miller is willing to consider the writings of Williams. In the preface to his book, Williams declares that his first aim is "to outline a new sub-science that shall be known as the Theory of Investment Value and that shall comprise a coherent body of principles like the Theory of Monopoly, the Theory of Money, and the Theory of International Trade, all branches of the larger science of Economics."[13]

In his seminal text, Williams addresses topics including long- and short-term interest rates, liquidity, uncertainty and risk, the future of investment rates, the likelihood of inflation, how markets arrive at stock prices, the relationship between commodity and security prices, and the impact of taxes. Like his contemporary, Ben Graham, he explains that "If a man buys a security below its investment value he need never lose, even if its price should fall at once, because he can still hold for income and get a return above normal on his cost price; but if he buys it at above its investment value, his only hope of avoiding a loss is to sell to someone else."[14]

Williams's book is highly technical—overly technical, in fact— and involves a fair amount of math, some for use in the evaluation of specific stocks. Williams recognized this as a problem and wrote, "The mathematics is not to be considered as a drawback to the analysis, however, nor as a method of reasoning which serious students can afford to neglect. Quite the contrary! The truth is that the mathematical method is a new tool of great power whose use promises to lead to notable advances in investment analysis."[15]

According to Williams's way of thinking, "Valuation is determined by the relation between a stock price and the present value of the free cash the business will generate over one's forecast time horizon." His book also introduced the dividend-discount model and cemented in place the definition of value as the "discounted present value of future cash flows."

Most contemporary investors, Buffett among them, utilize a variation of the dividend-discount model. Williams's concept that the investment value of a stock is the present worth of all the dividends that could be paid on it became the foundation for contemporary investment theory. For the word *dividend,* substitute a mental picture of all the cash that will be available at the end of a reporting period either (1) to distribute to shareholders as dividends, (2) to pay down debt, (3) to develop the business further, or (4) to acquire other businesses.

When it comes to bonds or other debt instruments, Williams defines the investment value as the present worth of its future coupons and principal. In the case of both stocks and bonds, an adjustment must be made on the inflation effect for expected changes in the purchasing power of money. Then the investor takes into account the interest rate the investor otherwise would be able to demand with minimum risk.

DISCOUNTING TO PRESENT VALUE

Miller is among myriad professional investors who use the equation called discounted cash flow to determine the correct price to be paid for current earning power. The equation allows an investor to plug in the future earnings of the security, the discount rate, and the time period involved, to come up with the present value or worth.

To achieve the needed figures, Miller estimates future cash flows and discounts them back to the present. The tricky part of the process is determining the consistency and stability of those cash flows into the future. The discount rate Miller uses depends on the type of company under scrutiny. The faster a company grows, the higher the rate he cranks into his calculations. When analyzing America Online, Miller cut himself considerable slack by using a discount rate as high as 30 percent. That's about three times what he might use for slower-growing companies. The higher discount rate builds that ever-important margin of safety.

In this regard, Miller is similar to Warren Buffett, who also prefers companies with consistent cash flow. Buffett feels safe with businesses such as Coca-Cola and Gillette because their cash flow streams are likely to be steady and predictable over time. Both Coke and Gillette have the industry dominance that allows them to price their product, which gives Buffett even greater confidence in strong and continuing cash flow.

Figuring discounted cash flow takes more work than some of the simple value tools such as price-to-earnings ratios and simply looking at past earnings trends. But it also lays down a clearer diagram of how such variables as future growth and interest rates will affect the value of the stock. Some investors use discounted cash flow as a way to obtain a second opinion, plugging in a current stock price to calculate how fast a company would need to grow to justify the current price.

The discounted cash flow model is one of the more sophisticated tools of the trade. Cash flow reflects money that is available for the company to redeploy in various possible ways, ways that if correctly chosen, will build value for the shareholder. The concept has been around for decades, with proxies such as the dividend-discount model for companies that have a long history of dividend payout. Investment bankers use similar models to price companies involved in mergers and acquisitions.

Despite the variations, the models attempt to achieve two goals: They estimate factors such as growth rates and predict profit margins to project how much money a company can generate in the future. The percentage of discount used usually depends on the interest rate available from a risk-free investment, the company's cost of capital, and the riskiness of the stock itself. Many professional investors use Bloomberg Financial Markets' off-the-shelf model, while others such as Miller build their own models. Bloomberg's service is considered very good, but it can cost $1,600 per month or more. There are a few web sites that offer the service free, and these are listed in Appendix 3 of this book.

LOOKING FORWARD

"Theoretically," says Bala Iyer, director of quantitative research at Banc One Investment Advisers, "the discounted-cash flow model is the perfect measure. The problem with it is that it relies a lot on forward-looking forecasts, and because of that it's susceptible to error."[16] The quality of the evaluation results depends on the quality of the projects that are loaded into the program.

Even Williams would agree that the problem comes with assessing the future free cash flow. He acknowledges that "It is a highly subjective and uncertain exercise."[17] But then, asks Miller, What's not susceptible to error? There are flaws to everything. The trick is to accept the vulnerability and work it into your calculations.

Miller recognizes the dilemma as well. The key to his process is trying to buy things at discounts to intrinsic business value, which from a theoretical standpoint is the present value of the future free cash flows. On the other hand, he looks for every kind of confirmation of his analysis. "Since the future free cash flows are unknown, it has to be estimated across a wide variety of scenarios," he explains. "We use a multi-factor valuation approach. We use historic valuation metrics where things have traded from both a company basis and from an industry standpoint. We are looking for things that are statistically cheap. There are a whole lot of things that go into the overall process."[18]

Another problem with the discount to future value model is that it is not suitable for short-term investment decisions—it focuses on long-term value. Just because a model shows that a stock is worth say $100 doesn't mean the stock will trade for that price anytime soon. Also, focusing on numbers alone can cause an investor to overlook a company with excellent business prospects. It probably would have always shown Microsoft as an overvalued stock. Discounted cash flow is a moving target, so any time there is some major news in interest rates or news related to the stock itself, the model needs to be run again.

A case in point: One of the reasons the technology sector became so extremely overvalued in the late 1990s, explains Miller, is

"XYZ Company, an optical network provider, was trading at a 25× P/E. Taking into account the capital needs and cash flow characteristics of the company, let's say that this 25 multiple discounts 25 percent growth for three years, followed by a return to a normalized growth rate of 12 percent. Optical networks, however, are experiencing explosive demand. It becomes clear to investors that the company can grow at, say, 35 percent for five years, before falling back to the 12 percent normalized rate, so the P/E expands to discount that future, and now it trades at 50×. This would be a reasonable valuation if in fact the company can turn in this growth over this period. However, let's say that the stock continues to climb and now trades at a P/E multiple of 150×. In order for investors to make an acceptable return buying the stock at this price, the company would have to grow at the faster rate for an even longer period, say 10 years. Thus, investors have brought the excess return expected years down the road into the present. If investors begin to think that the growth prospects for the company are no longer so long-lived, and again begin thinking the higher rate is only going to last for three years, the P/E could easily drop back down to 50–60×, even without any change to the earnings estimates for the next twelve months. This is what is often happening when stocks go down 50 percent or more, and yet, looking at the earnings the company is reporting today, it appears that 'nothing has changed.'"[19]

because investors were willing to look far, far into the future, expecting optimistic results for years ahead. This forward-looking bias increased risk. Miller's assistant Lisa Rapuano provided an example of how it works:

When looking at trends in technology, then, is it possible to formulate scenarios 5 years out? "No," declares Miller. "It is difficult to make anything more than the vaguest generalization about technology over that time frame. Those generalizations would not be sufficient to specify particular portfolio commitments."[20]

VALUE AND THE ECONOMY

Miller does not invest specifically on economic factors, but clearly, economics figures into the various scenarios he sets up for stock evaluations. Miller says he pays a lot of attention to markets and interest rates. Gold, oil, and commodity prices are some of the indicators he watches for signs of potential inflationary pressure.[21] Rather than try to forecast interest rates, however, he studies the current economic environment and tries to adjust his thinking accordingly. This, says Miller, is an essential part of the valuation process. "The justifiable valuation of a market with 7 percent inflation is radically different from the valuation of a market with 2 percent inflation."[22]

The market can be directionally correct, says Miller, while cross sectionally inefficient, "meaning that the market will sometimes price individual securities incorrectly relative to others. In other words, the market as a whole is accurately priced, but its individual pieces [the separate stocks] sometimes get mispriced. Looking within a single industry, you might find one company at one price and a very similar company with a dramatically different price."[23]

With such discrepancies in mind, in nearly every Value Trust annual report to shareholders, Miller quotes the Austrian "ordinary language philosopher," Ludwig Wittgenstein: "When we think about the future of the world, we always have in mind its being at the place where it would be if it continued to move as we see it moving now. We do not realize that it moves not in a straight line . . . and that its direction changes constantly."[24]

Market inefficiencies can happen for two or more reasons: Investors react emotionally to news and therefore make mistakes and/or investors don't have enough information to make a sound decision. Because of this situation, some investors and fund managers are able to outperform their peers.

Value has traditionally had up and down years, as investors responded to market sentiment. After a poor showing in parts of the 1990s it made a sudden recovery in 2001 when tech and Internet stocks collapsed, reminding investors that there remained a strong and vibrant world outside the computer and off the Internet. Despite the recovery, the rise of tech stocks gave traditional value investors pause. Yes, the smokestack, metal-bending, old-economy stocks still had value, but the world is changing and rapid-fire innovation in technology and services is here to stay.

LOOKING AT EVERY ELEMENT

Bill Miller relies on the dividend-discount model as an important tool, but he does not hesitate to add on other techniques. The approach is highly statistical and one form of analysis doesn't take precedence over the others. Again, Miller is looking at the distribution of the results, always seeking a clustered group of results that indicates consensus. Author Robert Hagstrom describes Miller's investing style as a Rubik's Cube approach. "He enthusiastically examines every issue from every possible angle, from every possible discipline, to get the best possible description—or redescription—of what is going on."[25]

Miller seeks companies that are undervalued on a 5- to 10-year basis, but he also seeks those that are the best available buys. If he owns a stock that trades at a 10 percent discount to its intrinsic value, and then finds another stock that trades at a 40 percent discount to its intrinsic value, the one closer to its intrinsic value is replaced by the one with the deeper discount. The stock with the 40 percent discount gives him a greater risk-adjusted return over the forecast time horizon.

Miller and his people do everything they can to fully understand a company's real value. They talk to management, suppliers, competitors, and analysts. "Because we are long-term owners of these companies and don't blow out the stock because it misses a quarter or underperforms for x period of time, management tends to be more open with us than with other shareholders or analysts, in terms of talking about long-term business strategies and issues," says Miller.[26] An in-depth research process is used for all the mutual funds for which Miller is responsible.

THE MULTIFACTOR VALUATION METHOD

In judging corporate worth, "We use what we call a multifactor valuation methodology, which is a mouthful for saying we look at the value of the business every possible way we can," says Miller. "We use P/E, price-to-book, price–to–cash flow, but we adjust those numbers."[27]

"We do all the cross-sectional analyses of trying to figure out what the historic parameters have been. Most important, we do a scenario analysis of the business. We project cash flows out anywhere from five to ten years under a variety of scenarios. One scenario would be where the current growth rate continues. Another is where the company does a lot worse. Another is where it does better. We then try to figure out what we call the 'central tendency of business value.' Each scenario analysis gives us a different number and then we see how those numbers cluster. If they all cluster around the same thing, then we have a pretty high confidence in the particular valuation range."[28]

"For new companies like AOL or Amazon we will use multiple scenarios with different endpoints, varying growth rates and a range of discount rates to get a sense of the risk/reward under different outcomes. We will also do comparative analyses of

> *companies with similar economic models. [In his
> books and classes, Graham did something similar,
> comparing the numbers and situations of two or
> three business competitors to determine which
> would be the best buy.] But the assumption or
> analysis of the comparative model is important."* [29]

How does Miller evaluate Internet companies with no revenue and no profit? Again, he uses multiple factors and scenarios; however, "Many of these companies we are not able to value because it's not clear what the long-term economic model is."[30]

Though Miller says his valuation process is not "overly mathematical," it does rely strongly on figures, because all businesses are mathematical. There is no other way of measuring profitability, says Miller.

NUMBERS ARE NOT ENOUGH

Because Miller realizes small mistakes can balloon up to huge errors when making projections, a formulaic approach alone is insufficient. That's where the intellectualization enters the picture. Research on the impact of technology on society, complex system studies, and visits to company chief executives to ask questions, especially about allocation of capital, all come into play. For these reasons, Miller considers nonmathematical factors. His most successful stocks, Miller says, have the following characteristics:

- They tend to have low valuations and are trading way down from their prior highs because of some problem, perceived or real. In ideal circumstances, the problem will be temporary and self-correcting.
- They are leaders in their industries. This leadership often gives a company "franchise value" to its products or company

name. Bruce C.N. Greenwald, professor of finance and asset management at Columbia University, says the "franchise value" approach is a beautiful match within the value framework. "Any service company with a great franchise, such as Wal-Mart [Stores Inc.] can be a lot less volatile than a manufacturing company."[31]

- They have managements who actually care about shareholder value. Miller explains that "It's about the ability of management to make right decisions as they build the business. If we didn't believe management was building value into a business, we wouldn't own it."[32]

- They have a fundamental economic model where they can earn above their cost of capital.[33] "Companies that grow are usually more valuable than companies that don't," explains Miller. "If a company earns below its cost of capital, though, then the faster it grows, the less it's worth. Companies that earn returns on capital above their cost of capital create value; those that earn below it destroy value. Those that earn results equal to the cost of capital grow value at the rate they add capital."[34]

These factors translate to the old adage, buy the company, not the stock. "Where our approach diverges from others is that we tend to actually invest in these businesses as opposed to trading stocks," Miller says. "In my judgment, many people who call themselves value investors neither value businesses nor invest in companies."[35]

RISK ASSESSMENT

Risk assessment is one of the most challenging aspects of money management. The managers of Long Term Capital Management were some of the brainiest people in the investment world, but they created a crisis, explains Miller, because they used linear models and were insufficiently aware of the model risk. LTCM managers relied too much on historical correlations. "The map isn't the territory," he cautions. "Maps leave a lot of detail out." True, you check a map if you want to know where the towns and water are, and if you're driving, where the roads go. But until we lift technology to Harry Potter dimensions, maps are static.

Miller points out that despite the most diligent research and analysis, something completely unexpected could happen at any time to change the direction of the market or the price of a specific company. This uncertainty is inevitable when market prices reflect news as it happens. For this reason, he looks at a huge mosaic of facts in an attempt to identify patterns.

Miller assesses risk in relation to the potential for long-term loss of capital on a stock-by-stock basis. He takes risk into account on a total portfolio basis in terms of volatility relative to the market and relative to the expectation of one's share. How do most other people assess risk? Miller has strong opinions about this, asserting that most people are risk-averse. "Psychological testing has established that for most of us, the pain of losing an amount of money is greater than the pleasure of winning that same amount of money," he explains.[36]

Say an investor puts $100,000 into a stock and gets a 20 percent return, realizing more than a $20,000 gain. Along with his profits, he gets a sense of pride and accomplishment. If he loses 20 percent, again the repercussions are more than monetary. He experiences remorse, shame, and grief. Since these feelings are felt more deeply than pride, there is a tendency to avoid situations in which the chances of both occurring are equal.

To illustrate the way that media coverage amplifies these feelings, Miller offers the example of an investor who bought a stock on Monday, then on Tuesday became engrossed in the television coverage of the O.J. Simpson trial. During the trial, the investor's stock declined, but the investor didn't react because she didn't know what happened. "If you missed the news until Wednesday, when the stock had recovered, you are much less likely to sell it then, even though the fundamentals are the same as the day before. That is myopic loss aversion at work."[37]

Investors are highly reactive to news, and because business news sources in print, television, radio, and on the Internet have proliferated in the past decade, investor trading stoked by information over-load has become almost frenzied. "The more short-term-oriented one is (the more 'myopic'), the greater one's willingness to react to the risk of loss," Miller observes.[38]

Since, on average, a dollar invested in stocks has returned, after in-flation, about 7 percent per year for more than 70 years, an investor is better off just picking a good-quality company and sticking with it. Professor Richard Thaler of the University of Chicago, after extensive research, is so convinced that the avalanche of information sweeping down on the investor does more harm than good, that he has pro-posed that universities not give faculty and employees reports on how their retirement funds are performing. For most investors, says Thaler, the appropriate advice is "don't just do something, sit there."[39]

A DEEPER REALITY

Because they are aware of how quickly and completely either mar-kets or stock prices can change, Miller's analysts reevaluate the companies they follow when quarterly earnings come in and any time there is significant news affecting the company or its industry. To make the analysts' work more challenging, the search is always on for companies that are cheaper than the companies the fund al-ready owns.

Miller says other value investors rely too much on "simplistic" tools and mathematical shortcuts that he considers merely "a way to get at a deeper reality," not an end in themselves. For example, many value investors sell too soon, and thus miss the best gains. What oth-ers do, he says, is look at historical trading patterns, then try to pick stocks based on historical relationships. "Then they trade out of them when they hit some other metric that relates to the historical trading pattern."[40] This type of investor does not grasp the notion that (1) fair value is time sensitive and (2) a strong, expanding busi-ness will continue to grow in value, even if the stock is no longer cheap on a price-to-earnings basis.[41]

CHAPTER 4

PORTFOLIO MANAGEMENT

You can observe a lot by just watchin'.

Yogi Berra

In his debut letter to shareholders, written for the March 31, 1991, Value Trust annual report, Bill Miller pointed out the challenge of portfolio management, at the same time throwing a punch at the increasing number of people who consider investing a rather exciting game of chance. Investment management, he said, at one time consisted of buying and holding stocks and bonds of investment grade. Preservation of capital was paramount; income and growth were to be desired. Performance was measured, if at all, over extremely, long periods of time. No thought was given to outguessing the stock market.

"Investing was serious business, not a game. 'Playing the market' was used to describe those whose investment purposes were not entirely serious, were perhaps even a bit frivolous. Dabbling in stocks was a pastime, not a profession for market 'players.' " There was a group of well-known characters, including Jesse Livermore, the notorious "Bet a Million" Gates, Arthur Cutten, and the Fisher brothers, who did gamble in the market, but there was an unmistakable moral and social distinction between them and the respected bankers who were the caretakers of wealth.

"That distinction became blurred," said Miller, "as Adam Smith recounts [in his book *The Money Game*] in the 1960s when the cult of performance first took hold. Just as Nixon declared in 1971, 'we are all Keynesians now,' portfolio managers are all performance driven now, since investable funds chase past performance records, and a portfolio manager without funds to manage is just expensive overhead."[1]

CALCULATING THE ODDS

Miller decided early in his career that trying to anticipate the direction of the stock market and invest according to a predicted outcome was not a smart game plan. And yet, like many investors, he found the parallels between gambling and investing lurking in the back of his mind. "The rewards of consistently beating the house at the casino or of regularly beating the market are substantial," he once wrote.

Back in the 1980s Miller read a book called *The Eudaemonic Pie* about a group of physicists and computer scientists who schemed to break the bank in Las Vegas. Their method was to build a computer into a player's shoe that could use statistics to predict what numbers and colors the roulette ball would land on. It was a harebrained scheme that didn't work, but what interested Miller most was that some of these probability experts abandoned their professions and became money managers.

Miller himself couldn't resist contemplating the odds of the stock market. In 1990, he wrote:

"*We* will not attempt to predict the market, except to note that the odds on its being higher in any 12 month period are about 66 percent since 1926. In the past 50 years the odds are better, *nearly 75 percent. The house advantage for investors in stocks has been 10.1 percent per year since 1926. In order to maximize the probabilities of long-term success, we intend, like the Eudaemons, to avoid betting on improbable outcomes. We will continue to look for sound companies whose shares can be purchased at discounts to what our analyses indicate they are worth, managed by people we can trust."[2]*

DECONSTRUCTING THE S&P 500

Miller makes a science of deconstructing the S&P, studying its moves the way a baseball coach studies game tapes. Why, he has asked himself, does the S&P 500 outperform 95 percent of all mutual fund managers when the committee that chooses the stocks in the index doesn't try to outperform anything? They simply try to select stocks that represent the overall U.S. economy, thus reflecting the condition of the market. They also seek companies with a leadership role in an industry, niche, or sector that have been around for an adequate time, have sufficient trading liquidity, and have financial traits that indicate they'll survive for 10 years or more.

S&P managers do replace stocks, but only for specific reasons. A company goes out when it is bought out, and a new stock is added to fill the slot. If a company changes so much that it no longer represents the economy, it can be tossed off the index. It was for this reason that Woolworth was written out of the S&P 500 and AOL replaced it.

Even so, "It's not the stock selection," says Miller, "it is the S&P's money management strategy. It's long-term, has low turnover, is tax-efficient, and doesn't change company and industry weightings. It just lets them evolve."[3] When money managers lag indexes, it is often due to the outperformance of the very large capitalization issues that dominate the averages compared to the generally smaller companies that make up most fund portfolios.[4]

Miller reached the conclusion that it's usually a mistake to continually fiddle with the mix of stocks in a portfolio to achieve some ideal balance. "The S&P doesn't come out and say, 'Microsoft is the biggest company, so let's cut it back.' They let their winners run. Technology and financial services together were 5.5 percent of the S&P 35 years ago. Now they are more than 40 percent."[5] This reflects what occurred in the world and what index managers allowed to happen in the S&P 500.

Buffett follows a similar strategy. He doesn't keep buying and selling Coca-Cola for the sake of balancing Berkshire's portfolio. He has learned to buy quality stocks and to hold on as long as they still have growth potential. When he decides there is some fundamental reason to sell, he then sells.

If the S&P 500 is managed so intelligently, why not just put your money in the S&P—buy an index fund or purchase Standard & Poor's Depositary Receipts (Spiders)? Not such a bad idea, says Miller. "The S&P is a wonderful thing to put your money in. If somebody said, 'I've got a fund here with a really low cost, that's tax efficient, with a 15 to 20 year record of beating almost everybody,' why wouldn't you own it?"[6]

This is not to imply, however, that to outperform the S&P 500, a portfolio should be exactly like it. Passive management of that sort would result in merely keeping up with the market, not outperforming it. In general, Legg Mason's asset allocation strategy is to own about 11 percent of dynamic growth stocks, representing the high-growth segment of the market; 43 percent global franchise stocks, representing the large-cap growth segment; and 46 percent to traditional value, encompassing higher dividend yielding stocks and small- and mid-cap stocks.

DEFINING THE MILLER STYLE

There are two basic types of value funds: a disciplined fund and a subjective fund. Managers of disciplined funds buy stocks sticking to the traditional mechanical criteria such as price-to-book, price-to-earnings, or price-to-sales ratios. Such a fund typically would acquire stocks with P/B ratios that fall in the lowest 30 percent of the range of New York Stock Exchange stocks, usually a P/B of less than 1.5.

Managers of subjective funds use these tools as well, but invest greater faith in their own judgment. If the manager's analysis says a $10 stock will be worth $50 in the future, then the security qualifies as a value buy. Some investors insist that Miller's fund belongs in the subjective category, but in fact, that seems like a misjudgment. Miller clearly uses the disciplined approach, activating analytical tools more precise and sophisticated than those taught to most value investors. The difference is that he doesn't stop there. He continues to examine investment ideas from every angle imaginable. The style Miller uses to manage Value Trust has three main components: (1) careful attention to value, (2) focus on a relatively small number of carefully selected stocks, and (3) low turnover of fund shares.

ATTENTION TO VALUE

Miller's critics claim that his fund should not carry the name *value* in its title, and even suggest that the Securities and Exchange Commission should instruct him to rename the fund. Miller doubts that will happen. "The name Value Trust is not a description of the type of companies that we own; it's a description of our objective in delivering value to our shareholders. If they're going to determine what counts as value, they'll never find any justification from any finance textbook or anybody who has written about value or valuation."[7]

Furthermore, Miller sees a false distinction between the concepts of value and growth:

"*People believe that somehow or other there are characteristics of companies that make them growth or value. I believe that growth-value distinctions really describe the styles of money managers, not the characteristics of companies. Value managers put valuation as the critical driver in their style. Growth managers focus on growth and underweigh valuation.*"[8]

Unfortunately, Miller says, value investors, especially in the past decade, have avoided technology because they haven't taken the time or effort to understand it. Additionally, they've put too much emphasis on historical information that has little impact on the current environment. "That's not because it's a different world or new era, but because the valuation metrics they are using came from an era of much higher inflation and higher interest rates. We now have a low inflation, low interest rate environment, yet they haven't adjusted their models."[9]

In his search for new acquisitions, Miller uses computer screens as a way to sort companies' characteristics. All of the different valuations in his multidisciplinary model must confirm each other before he buys a stock. He calls this consensus "central tendency valuation."[10]

For the most part, Miller's model turns up larger companies than those usually found in a classic value fund such as Vanguard Value Index. Legg Mason's median market cap is around $44 billion versus $34 billion for Vanguard. Although the numbers constantly fluctuate, Vanguard's P/E typically is 25.1 compared to 32.5 for Value Trust. Vanguard's P/B is 3.7 versus 10.4 for Value Trust.

ATTENTION TO FOCUS

Value Trust is a relatively limited fund in terms of the number of stocks it contains. In most years, its portfolio contains about 40 stocks (sometimes as many as 48), and typically about half of that is invested in its 10 largest holdings.[11]

Miller says he doesn't need any greater diversification because his team has done such in-depth research that they have great confidence in their holdings. It isn't possible, he says, to do that level of research on 300 companies. "T. Rowe Price once said he would have done better in his first stock fund if he had only hung on to its original position in IBM," Miller remarks.[12]

ATTENTION TO LOW TURNOVER

Miller is wary of turnover. Through the entire first quarter of 1995, he didn't add or subtract a single stock from Value Trust's portfolio—which is not unusual for value investors such as Warren Buffett, but is quite unusual for mutual fund managers.[13]

His critics say Miller has a tendency to get too close to his stocks and stay with them perhaps longer than he should. For example, *Smart Money* noted, Bank One was down 40 percent (in July 2000) since Miller bought in. Most investors would have sold out and cut their losses. He still owned nearly 14 million shares in 2001 although the shares were still trading in a fairly flat range between the mid 20s and mid 30s per share.

Like almost all investors, professional or home-style, Miller occasionally picks a klunker. He conceded that Waste Management was a "disaster" for Value Trust in 1999. Waste Management got clobbered after Miller bought it, falling more than 70 percent. He began buying the shares in the low $50 range, then watched the share price slump to below $20. In hindsight, Miller said he wished he had put greater weight on an early warning: cash flow that appeared low relative to reported earnings. Instead, he accepted Waste Management's explanation of unusual seasonal factors.[14] Moreover, after assigning a member of his team to reevaluate the stock, Miller decided the long-term prospects were bright and continued to acquire. He was right. The entire story of Waste Management is told in Chapter 7.

Early in 1999, Miller bowed to another miscalculation, dumping shares of PennCorp Financial Group, an insurance company. He dubbed it "Penn Corpse" after the shares lost nearly all their value. He also admits to some "errors of omission," such as Wal-Mart. In the late 1980s, he decided he liked the stock on the basis of its cash flow, but wanted the price to drop a half point before buying. Instead, Wal-Mart kept going up, and he decided to buy something else. Since that time, Wal-Mart rose fivefold, though it's mostly been moving sideways since 2000.[15]

Investors in Legg Mason's funds receive tax advantages from Miller's goal of owning stocks for the long term, but there are other advantages to shareholders as well. The longer holding period allows Miller to build relations with management and to more clearly perceive a company's direction. He has a special interest in how management plans to use its cash to expand market share. Understanding a business and its industry is a key part of Miller's strategy.

Usually Miller holds on to his stocks an average of 5 years and sometimes as long as 10 years while the average large-cap value fund rotates through its entire portfolio every 18 months. The turnover in Value Trust has been running between 10 and 15 percent a year in recent years, which is one of the lowest in the industry. "We really are investors, not traders," Miller explains.

THE ROLE OF CAPITAL GAINS

When it becomes necessary to take capital gains, Miller hears about it from his shareholders. While Miller works hard to keep fund turnover low, there are times when change seems almost unavoidable. For example, in the summer of 2000, after Miller had shifted emphasis from tech back to traditional value, he needed to dispose of topped-out tech stocks such as Dell and America Online and replace them with a new group of undervalued stocks.

For most investors the tax bite for long-term capital gains was 20 percent. If a person owned 100 shares of Value Trust and the distribution was $6, the investor would owe the tax collector $120. For those who had been in the fund for 10 years and had enjoyed Value Trust's 21.2 percent 10-year annualized return, the tax might only seem fair.

The deepest pain taxwise is reserved for recent investors. An unnecessary large sale of highly valued stock, notes Miller, would be unfair to those shareholders who weren't in the fund long enough to participate in the gain, but would be liable for the taxes.

Worse yet, the new investor, when he bought his shares, would have no way to know what he was walking into. This type of dilemma is avoidable for a while, but the only secure investment gain comes when interest or dividends are paid, or when a security is sold. At some point, Miller has to weigh fund performance against tax consequences and make tough decisions.

SELL CRITERIA

What would make Miller decide to sell a stock? "If it looks as if your valuation work is wrong, or if the stock gets to a price that's dramatically above its business value, as [AOL] did in March and April of 1999," he replies.[16]

This exact situation in 2000 motivated Miller to sell part of his position in Dell. "That's when you get to the point of balancing risk and taking taxes into consideration," Miller explains. "We have billions of dollars in gains in both Dell and AOL. We want to avoid delivering massive capital gains to our shareholders if we can. We will never sacrifice returns so people don't have to pay taxes, but we're trying to maximize their after-tax rates of return."[17]

Miller practices a three-part sell discipline. He sells if

1. The stock is fairly priced. When a company has achieved its fair price (or full valuation), Miller cannot expect to earn an excess return by owning the company over a multi-year period in the future.

2. He finds a better bargain. Miller tries to remain fully vested in stocks. Because his cash holdings are fairly small, if a better bargain comes along, he must sell his least attractive holding and make a replacement.

3. The investment situation changes. There may be a change in a company's basic business model, such as a shift in government regulation or permanent alterations in market conditions.

*M*iller will continue to own a company as long as he is confident of the business value and management's ability to convert from undervalue to full valuation. "As long as we trust management and believe it's dealing with us in a fair way, we will hold the stock. Circus Circus [now called Mandalay Resort Group] is a good example. We owned it for three years, and it did nothing but go down. As it turns out, we were too optimistic about the environment in Las Vegas and how that would develop. Even though the stock performed poorly, we kept buying it because the stock price declined more than the business values."[18] Three years after Miller bought it in 1996, he was vindicated. Mandalay shares doubled in price.

STRAYING FROM TRADITION

Miller stretches beyond the traditional value practices and principles by incorporating modern portfolio theory (MPT) into his management style. MPT is a strategy by which risk/reward relationships are established for individual stocks, and then the portfolio itself is constantly scrutinized to make sure the collection of securities presents the lowest possible risk for the highest possible return.

Modern portfolio theory involves four basic steps:

1. *Security valuation*, or establishing a universe of assets in terms of expected return and expected risk
2. *Asset allocation decisions*, or determining how assets are to be distributed among classes of investments, such as stocks and bonds
3. *Portfolio optimization*, or reconciling risk and return in the selection of securities to be held in the portfolio, including which stock offers the best return for an acceptable level of determining risk.
4. *Performance measurement*, or allocating each stock's performance into systematic market-related classifications and analyzing the stock's contribution to returns.

For more details on security evaluation and risk assessment, turn back to Chapter 3. As for asset allocation and performance measurement, read on.

ASSET ALLOCATION

Miller takes reasonable care not to be overloaded in any one market sector, stressing the importance of balance. For example, in 1990, Miller had just under 85 percent of Value Trust's funds in stocks, but no single industry sector had more than 15 percent of the funds. About 15 percent of the funds were in banking, finance and insurance represented 7 percent each, utilities 5.4 percent, and the remainder were grouped in units of less than 5 percent. As mentioned earlier, Miller is not afraid to allow his winners to continue to the point that they make up an ever larger percentage of his holdings. In 2000, another sample year, 96.6 percent of Value Trust's funds were vested in stocks, but the spread was far different.

Nearly 29 percent were in technology, thanks to holdings in quickly rising stocks such as Dell and America Online. Nearly 28 percent were in financials, but that was mainly because Value Trust now lumped banks, savings and loans, insurance and brokerage companies under that heading.

In 1991, when market participants were enamored with cyclical stocks, Miller noted that every year some different group of stocks becomes the rage and rises simply because people think it will. "Last year small stocks starred, led by the biotechs, which rose over 100 percent, and small stock managers with heavy exposure to medical technology were heroes. Biotechnology stocks this year are the market's worst performers falling on the average over 40 percent from their peaks. The risk in the group was particularly evident in Centocor, one of last year's darlings. The FDA failed to approve their main product, stunning most observers, who had already factored hundreds of millions of dollars of sales into their projections. The stock collapsed from a high of over $60 per share to a current price of $12; its market value fell from over $2 billion to just over $400 million."[19]

AN AVERSION TO CYCLICALS

Another aspect of Miller's allocation philosophy is his distaste for cyclicals, which he seldom purchases. As he puts it:

"*Most cyclicals operate in undifferentiated commodity businesses with little or no control over product pricing, have fluctuating and unpredictable earnings and cash flow streams, no significant competitive advantages, poor returns on capital, and have little or no free cash flow after taxes and capital expenditures. Their reported earnings do bounce around a lot and usually go up as the economy improves. But to earn above average returns in these kinds of stocks requires one to buy and sell at precisely the right time, such timing having little to do with careful analysis of business values and everything to do with guessing inflection points in the economy and market sentiment.*[20]

Their unique qualities make cyclical stocks poor long-term investments, which is precisely the reason Miller tends to steer clear of them. Cyclicals, he explains, typically have spurts of strong performance as the economy snaps back from a recession, and markets envision improved earnings.

But, "as the economy expands, these stocks lag, even as earnings begin to materialize. Finally, they fall sharply when the market expects recession and the consequent collapse in their earnings. Over a full economic cycle the performance is usually uninspiring, and over the longer term, often abysmal. General Motors sells today [Spring 1993] for a lower price than it did in the 1960s, and airlines have earned no more money in aggregate since Kitty Hawk."[21]

Despite his aversion to cyclicals, Miller will in fact buy them if first, they are cheap for some fundamental reason aside from their earnings cycles, or second, they offer a specific advantage over other stocks. Consumer cyclicals typically account for about 13 percent of Value Trust's assets. He often owns automobile manufacturing companies and has held General Motors since the mid-1990s. Only one reporting period—fiscal year 2000–2001—did GM let him down, and that year it was off by 37.4 percent.

In the early 1990s Miller made profits in bank stocks. Banks had been wrung out by a series of adverse events and were selling at the lowest valuations in their history. Citicorp (now called Citigroup) is a classic example of a quality bank that lost excessive share price value during this episode. Nevertheless, capital was expanding rapidly, industry consolidation was underway, and Miller saw great prospects for acquisitions, less competition, and dividend growth. He favors banks because these financial institutions, unlike other cyclicals, have a return on capital greater than their cost of capital. In other words, they actually earn a return for their shareholders on the money that has been invested in the business. Many other cyclicals actually erode shareholder value. Only companies that earn a return over their cost of capital are suitable as long-term investments.

PERFORMANCE MEASUREMENT

Since its inception in 1982, Value Trust has earned an annual compounded return for shareholders of 18.24 percent. The fund's performance uses the S&P 500 as a formal benchmark, but Miller has suggested that the fund's total return might also be compared with the total return of the Value Line Geometric Average (commonly called the Value Line Index), an index of approximately 1,700 stocks. You might think that the S&P 500 and the Value Line Index would report similar gains. In fact, they are surprisingly far apart. In the year ending March 31, 2001, Value Trust was off by 9.99 percent, S&P down by 21.68 percent, and the Value Line Index was a negative 13.86 percent. Miller says that the Lipper Growth Fund Index probably is the best general benchmark, since it consists of actively managed funds with similar long-term objectives, "albeit dissimilar styles of achieving those objectives."[22]

REPORTED RETURNS

Some investors have complained over the years that their personal experience with Legg Mason Value Trust was not as cheery as was reported in the media and touted in Legg Mason advertisements. Miller says this very well may be true for several reasons:

- The way that average annual returns are computed tends to smooth out variations in the fund's returns, so they may differ somewhat from actual year-to-year results.
- Reported returns include reinvested dividends.
- An individual's returns will depend on the actual dates he or she bought into or sold out of the fund.

Furthermore, Miller admits, even though Value Trust is "one of the few funds to have outperformed the S&P 500 since our inception in early 1982, and one of only about two dozen to have outpaced that index in each of the past five calendar years, we have had periods of underperformance."[23]

At the end of 2001, for example, Value Trust was a laggard when compared with other funds of similar composition—i.e., those emphasizing large-cap value stocks. After the tech market decline of earlier in the year and the September 11 terrorist attack on the United States, the fund's assets fell from around $12 billion to $8.9 billion and it was underperforming its peers by 70 percent for the year. Similar funds were down only 6.7 percent in 2001. Even though Value Trust recently (2000) beat the S&P 500 for the eleventh consecutive year, it was ranked among the bottom 10 percent of large value portfolio funds, according to the fund tracking service, Morningstar Inc.

REALISTIC EXPECTATIONS

When judging performance, those pesky mistaken assumptions discussed in Chapter 2 can take multitudes of forms, especially in the world of Wall Street. Take the assumptions surrounding market returns: The year 2000, after 5 years of record-breaking stock market returns—annual averages of about 25 percent—was a disappointment to many investors, especially those who had never met up with a flat or declining market. The Dow, NASDAQ, and S&P 500 all lost value that year. A survey of investors by the Securities Industry Association about that time showed that investors expected to earn 33 percent per year, on average, despite the fact that stock markets have only averaged about 10 percent annually over the past 70 years.

Some fund investors have expressed disappointment in Miller's performance in the years that all the indexes were down, even though Value Trust lost less money than its benchmark index. Fidelity Investment's Peter Lynch has little patience with people who think that markets will go up forever. They should understand that markets sometimes go down, Lynch says, and even the best fund managers can't change that. "We try and slow people down and say, 'You spend four hours [researching] a round-trip ticket to Bermuda. You should spend some more time seeing what the hell you're doing [with your investments]."[24]

KEEP AS MUCH MONEY IN STOCKS AS POSSIBLE

It makes sense to be as fully vested in stocks as possible, says Lynch, especially if you can lock in to those companies with reliable, steady growth of profits. "For people to say, 'I'm down 20 percent in the S&P 500. Therefore, call my aunt, call my grandmother, call the kids and get out of the IRAs.' Historically it's wrong. I don't know about [the direction of] the next 2,000 points for the market, but the next 10,000 will be up. It's called corporate profits. Profits grow at 9 percent per year and double every eight years, quadruple every 16 years, go up eight-fold every 24 years, go up 16-fold every 30. That's the map. That's what you have to get into people's heads. There's a reason why stocks go up; it's called profit growth."[25]

NO PERFORMANCE ANXIETY

Miller says he feels no pressure to live up to the expectations of investors who see him as a superstar. But, he says,

"*I* do have concern that shareholders are buying the fund not fully understanding our strategy. Shareholders who chase performance are not the kind of shareholders who are most suitable for this fund. There are funds set up to shoot the lights out every year. That's their job. We're trying to earn the highest possible risk-adjusted returns for our clients on a long-term basis using a valuation-driven methodology. We're not going to change our strategy or style if we underperform a bit, and we undoubtedly will underperform. If people are surprised by that, they should look at another fund."[26]

This said, Miller and his team are highly competitive, both with other mutual funds and within their own organization. Each year, employees in Legg Mason's mutual fund unit stage a competition in which they choose a small number of stocks from the fund's full list and stick with their picks for a year. The person with the highest performance wins. More than once, the winner has been an administrative assistant.

██████ FIXED-INCOME SECURITIES

Typically, Miller places a limited amount of Value Trust's funds into bonds or other fixed-income securities. In any pool of funds it is necessary to have a place to park cash while either waiting or accumulating for some better investment. Miller tends to park as little as possible, though the amounts he has set aside in this fashion have varied from 10.8 percent in 1998 to a scant 1.1 percent in 2001.

Miller asks why long-term investors would own bonds at all, considering that averaging over a 70-year period, a dollar invested in bonds returns less than 1 percent annually, while stocks return about 7 percent. His answer: Individual investors tend to have more of their funds in bonds than stocks because stocks are more volatile, and therefore more nerve-wracking to own. The bond market, says Miller, suffers from a malady called "opsophobia: fear of prosperity."[27]

This not to say that he never invests in bonds or bond-like securities. Miller is creative in the places he looks for value. In 1995, he decided that Argentina's U.S.-guaranteed Brady bonds were selling at much less than they were worth and made a major investment. The bonds tripled in 2 years and were sold before the Latin American economy crumbled again. The opportunity was "incredibly compelling," explains Lisa Rapuano. "When we see a gigantic misvaluation in the market, we'll do something like that, but we haven't done that often."[28]

██████ A SMALL NUMBER OF BIG WINS?

Back in the 1980s when Miller was director of research at Legg Mason, he put together a Thanksgiving list of 12 stock picks for the year ahead. This effort became an annual event, but was discontinued in the 1990s. "The list had a really good record of beating the market. The *Wall Street Journal* began to pick up on it in the early 1980s. They published our list on Thanksgiving Day." After the third year the list appeared, a reporter called Miller and said he'd analyzed the lists. He pointed out to Miller that for 1 year, if the top two stocks were thrown out, Miller would not have beaten the market. In another year, Miller only beat the market because he had one big takeover stock on the list. Miller replied, "If the assumption is we don't own the things that enable us to beat the market, then it follows that we won't beat the market. But we do own them."[29]

THE DANGER OF SUCCESS

As word of a fund's achievement spreads, new investors invariably are attracted to it and it increases in size. Miller often is asked the question: At what point will Value Trust, or any mutual fund for that matter, become too large to manage?

So far the problem has been self-resolving, since investors fled Value Trust—as if it were a tech or growth fund—when tech stocks took an end-of-the-century nosedive. However, the fund has grown considerably over the years and Miller has an idea of how big is too big. He tries to keep average assets under management roughly equivalent to the average market capitalization of the stocks he owns. If the fund has big capitalization, it begins to impact the company it owns and vice versa. Consider a small-cap fund with $500 million under management; a manager can't own companies with market capitalization much smaller than $500 million, or the single fund would own too much of the company. The impact cost would be too high if it bought or sold its holdings.

Although the Legg Mason Value Trust, primarily a domestic investment fund, grew from $800 million in 1990 to more than $12 billion in 2001, it is still small compared to Janus 20 ($15 billion), Vanguard Windsor II ($22 billion), Washington Mutual Investors ($48 billion), and so on. Fidelity Magellan is the world's largest mutual fund with approximately $78.8 billion in assets.

At a time when Value Trust had $13 billion in assets, its companies had an average market cap of about $50 billion. Using that as a measure, Miller could take in twice the amount of assets without impacting performance. "Another way to look at it is the S&P 500 has about $10 trillion in assets. The S&P 500, as you know, outperforms most managers most of the time. This means there's $10 trillion of assets under management that outperform almost everybody. But they own 500 stocks. We own 50 stocks. Therefore, we could theoretically outperform with $1 trillion, which is ten times what Fidelity Magellan has in it right now."[30]

CHAPTER 5

NEW ECONOMY VALUATION

You certainly look cool.	Mrs. Lindsay
You don't look so hot yourself.	Yogi Berra

On April 4, 2000, Miller spoke to students at Michael Mauboussin's securities analysis class at Columbia University. He told the class that technology stocks had soared like a runaway hot-air balloon, and although prices had come down to earth somewhat, there was a lot more fizzle ahead.

While the trauma to high-technology securities presented a problem to Miller, it also meant that his methodology would gain even greater respect than it had in the past.

"Valuations have not mattered in four or five years, and they have reached an extreme level," Miller said. "We've reached a period where valuation will begin to matter again, so we have begun reducing our technology weighting."[1]

Tech stocks were strong throughout the 1990s, but the real surge began in late 1998. At that time, a widespread belief developed that a new set of rules applied to these equities. Analysts predicted that there was virtually no limit to the sales and earnings gains that technology companies could generate. As for old-economy companies, they were advised either to go on line or close their doors.

In the late 1990s, Internet and cutting-edge telecommunications companies were clearly revolutionizing the world. The work they were doing was so radical that investors seemed to feel these pioneers deserved equally radical financial valuation methods. The tradition of securities analysis, with attention to assets, sales, earnings, and cash flow, were as old-fashioned as wooden bats. Revenue growth, web site traffic, and even spending patterns were the power behind the home runs.

NEW TECHNOLOGY, NEW ACCOUNTING

The general attitude was, "We've got a new technology, and therefore it's perfectly okay to have a new way of approaching the income statement and balance sheet," recalled Anthony Maracarco, a portfolio manager at the Babson Value Fund in Boston. Yet, explained Maracarco, reality eventually would take hold with investors. "Sooner or later you have to generate cash and if all you're doing is using cash, you can only play that game for so long."[2]

Despite pressure from every direction, many value investors refused to play in the high-tech arena. Even though she had admonished Miller as a traitor to the value camp for his interest in technology, mutual fund columnist Mary Rowland later complained about the way value investors viewed the Internet. "I was discouraged to learn that many of them don't view it at all," she wrote.[3]

Don Phillips, chief executive of Morningstar, the mutual fund rating service, expressed a similar concern. "It's quaint to say you don't invest in businesses you don't understand. But it's increasingly ridiculous to relegate all tech companies to that category." Phillips, who described himself as a value investor, took an even harder whack at the value crowd. "A friend of mine says that a good value manager doesn't buy stocks. He manages a kennel. I think value investing is at a crossroads."[4]

The fact that most value funds had minimal technology exposure was due to both lack of knowledge and to the extremely elevated prices that tech stocks traded for in relation to earnings or other fundamentals, contended Miller. "More often, though," he said, "the reason is lack of familiarity or an unwillingness to try to analyze what appears to be a complex group whose fundamentals often seem unpredictable."[5]

Yet in the 1990s, sound high-tech performers such as Sun Microsystems, EMC, and Oracle exhibited characteristics cherished by value seekers. They sold at single digit price-to-earnings multiples. But even at those low multiples, value managers shunned them.

Miller's own fund became one of the exceptions. Beginning in 1996, Value Trust had significantly greater weighting in tech than most value funds. In late 1999, Value Trust was weighted at 42 percent to 43 percent in those holdings. A few other value fund managers joined Miller in investing in tech stocks, including Bill Nygren at Oakmark Select and Mason Hawkins at Longleaf Partners.

MILLER STEPS TO THE PLATE

Miller explains his position as follows:

"*We believe and continue to believe that technology can be analyzed on a business basis, that intrinsic value can be estimated, and that using a value approach in the tech sector is a competitive advantage in an area dominated by investors who focus exclusively, or mainly on growth, and often ignored by those who focus on value.*"[6]

Miller points out, however, that there are vital, additional factors to be considered when contemplating high-technology investments. Working with Ernie Kiehne helped ground him in value fundamentals. But it was by following his own philosopher's bent, exploring futurist ideas discussed in Chapter 2—swarm intelligence, complex systems research, collective behavior, and other concepts at the Santa Fe Institute—that Miller developed a taste for Internet and technology stocks such as the fledgling America Online.

> "*A*lthough technology changes really rapidly," explains Miller, "it doesn't follow that such change is random or unpredictable. In many cases, it follows defined paths. Economists such as Brian Arthur and Hal Varian have explored the economics of technology and information-based businesses. Their work is accessible to anyone who will take time to study it."[7]

Still, technologies do sometimes emerge in mysterious ways. Take, for example, interactive videoconferencing: Businesses can get this cost-saving service via Integrated Services Digital Network (ISDN), but it isn't used much. Even in the twenty-first century, there is something about face-to-face contact that builds trust and cements deals. In addition to uncertainty as to what products will catch on, there remain questions about how the high-tech economy is structured. The markets themselves are more volatile and unpredictable than their low-tech counterparts, and there is enormous controversy about how to evaluate individual securities on a business basis.

ENTERING THE AGE OF TECHNOLOGY

Miller reminds us of what most of us already recognize—that we are in transition from a mass-production, commodity-manufacturing economy to an information-based, digital, high-tech economy. The future will be skewed toward the latter.

Clearly, radical shifts in the economy are nothing new. Every 50 to 100 years has seen deep and fundamental structural changes. In the 1700s, it was a shift from cottage industries to simple manufacturing; in the late 1700s, the Industrial Revolution, or steam power, took precedence. In the 1820s, international trade clambered to the top, and in the mid-1800s, the economy split into those who had capital and those who supplied labor. As the twentieth century began, mass production stepped into the spotlight. Each of these advances led to shifts in the means of production, and the character and basic operating rules of the economy.

What has happened in recent decades, says Miller, "is a lot like the change from an agrarian economy to an industrial economy. It didn't happen all at once; it happened very subtly, year after year, but the accumulated change was very large."[8]

This leads to an unavoidable truth: If an investor is going to follow the approach used so successfully by Graham, Buffett, Lynch, and the other notable value investors, if the goal is to buy a security as if you are buying the entire company, then it is necessary to understand something about the economics governing that company and the industry in which it operates.

Brian Arthur points out that in the winner-take-most market economy of knowledge based companies, "managing becomes rede fined as a series of quests for the next technological winner the next cash cow. The goal becomes the search for the Next Big Thing."[9]

WHO IS IN THE GAME

Arthur equates the high-tech atmosphere with a gambling casino with many playing tables. A player might sit at the Internet retailing table, the electronic banking table, or the brokerage service table. Then Arthur poses the question, "How much to play? You ask. Three billion, the croupier replies. Who'll be playing? We won't know until they show up. What are the rules? Those'll emerge as the game unfolds. What are my odds of winning? We can't say. Do you still want to play? High tech, pursued at this level, is not for the timid. In fact, the art of playing the tables in the Casino of Technology is primarily a psychological one. What counts to some degree—but only to some degree—is technical expertise, deep pockets, will, and courage. Above all, the rewards go to the players who are first to make sense of the new games looming out of the technological fog, to see their shape, to recognize them. Bill Gates is not so much a wizard of technology as a wizard of precognition, of discerning the shape of the next game."[10]

The old-economy era of diminishing returns encouraged optimizing strategies such as high-level management, cost cutting, and the like, but "you cannot optimize [those management factors] in the casino of increasing-returns games," continues Arthur. "You *can* be smart. You *can* be cunning. You *can* position. You *can* observe. But when the games themselves are not even fully defined, you cannot optimize. What you *can* do is adapt. Adaptation, in the proactive sense, means watching for the next wave that is coming, figuring out what shape it will take, and positioning the company to take advantage of it. Adaptation is what drives increasing-return businesses, not optimization."[11]

VAPORWARE

Psychological positioning in such scenarios becomes a consequential strategy. Under increasing returns, rivals will retreat in a market, not *just* if it is locked in, but also if they *believe* someone else will lock it in. Arthur says this is why "we see psychological jockeying in the form of preannouncements, feints, threatened alliances, technological preening, touted future partnerships, parades of vaporware [announcements of products that don't yet exist]. This posturing and puffing acts much as similar behavior does in a primate colony: it discourages competitors from taking on a potentially dominant rival. No moves need to be made in this strategy of pre-market face down. It is purely a matter of psychology."[12] As discomfiting as it might be, increasing returns do not lead to equilibrium but rather to instability: if a product or a company or a technology—one of many competing in a market—gets ahead by chance or by clever strategy, increasing returns can magnify this advantage, and the product or company or technology can go on to lock in the market," writes Arthur.[13]

This positive-feedback economics, explains Arthur, has parallels in modern nonlinear physics. Ferromagnetic materials, spin glasses, solid-state lasers, and other physical systems that consist of mutually reinforcing elements show similar properties. In some cases, small changes in properties or circumstances can dramatically alter the course of events. "They phase-lock into one of many possible configurations, small perturbations at the critical times influence which outcome is selected, and the chosen outcome may have higher energy—be less efficient—than other possible end-states. It finds parallels in modern evolutionary thinking as well. Small events, the mutations of history, are indeed often averaged away, but once in a while they become all-important in tilting parts of the economy into new structures and patterns that are then preserved and built upon in a fresh layer of development. The economy we have inherited is in part the result of historical chance."[14] One historical example is the development of the airplane. The Wright Brothers had many competitors all over the world, and the one with the most promise of success was John Montgomery, a professor in northern California. However, the 1906 San Francisco earthquake did so much damage to Montgomery's home and workshops that the Wrights gained an advantage of time. Two years after the earthquake, they ended up with the lion's share of credit, not to mention patents on fixed wing flight.

OLD TRUTHS

Hal Varian, who has published dozens of research papers in economic theory, econometrics, industrial organization, and the economics of information technology, has a somewhat different perspective on the new economy. To Varian's way of thinking, the economic principles haven't changed as much as Arthur believes.

Speaking to the National Press Club in Canberra, Australia, Varian said: "Some people argue that we do need a new economics to understand the new economy of bytes. We do have a new economy—there's no doubt huge economic forces are at work. But you don't need a new economics to understand the new economy. But you don't need to rely on the speculation of gurus. You can learn a lot from history and case studies and economic analysis."[15]

Varian contends that Internet commerce ignores established economic rules at its own peril. Some old truths—the rules of supply and demand and often, the principles of diminishing returns—remain intact. The Priceline.com, name-your-price web site, for example, was unable to change consumer behavior.

In his book, *Information Rules,* Varian used the Internet auction site eBay Inc. as an example. Its business model wasn't novel or new—it was simply an electronic classified advertising service. What made the site more relevant than the old model, a newspaper, was the enormously enlarged number of buyers and sellers. Pricing became more efficient due to higher volume and the business caught fire. Varian's advice to those hoping to replicate eBay's success? Look for a business like the classifieds that has worked in the past and figure out a way to reconfigure it to its best advantage using the Internet.

"Executives charged with rolling out cutting-edge software products or online versions of their magazines are tempted to abandon the classic lessons of economics, and rely instead on an ever-changing roster of trends, buzzwords and analogies that promise to guide strategy in the information age," he warns.[16] Varian advises people not to buy into that philosophy, and yet because there is so much to know and understand about the high-tech world, he encourages an expanded way of thinking. Some of his concepts are nearly identical to Arthur's.

In this new economy, for example, a brand name can be a benefit, as long as hubris doesn't cloud the picture. "A valuable brand name allows a company to command some premium, but won't guarantee the same prices or margins enjoyed before new information technologies arrived that caused per-copy and distribution costs to fall. In our experience, information providers with established brand names often hesitate to drop prices quickly enough to warn off potential entrants, perhaps because they think their brand name shields them from competition."[17]

Varian claims that companies that are slow to accept the inevitability that new technologies will force lower prices for basic information may find themselves rapidly losing market share on all fronts. CNET, a media company, has been able to avoid that trap. CNET has been a leader in the on-line news area precisely because they've been willing to experiment with new business models without having to worry about cannibalizing a print publication.[18] Even so, CNET's shares suffered in the Internet crash. In 1999 the shares traded as high as $79. By late 2001, its shares were trading at around $5.

As noted, Varian and Arthur agree on many key points. "The shared nature of information technology makes it critical to address issues of standardization and interoperability sooner rather than later," writes Varian. "Each consumer's willingness to use a particular piece of technology—such as the Internet—depends strongly on the number of other users. New communication tools, such as fax machines, VCRs and the Internet itself, have typically started out with long periods of relatively low use followed by exponential growth; this means that changes are much cheaper and easier to make in the early stages. Furthermore, once a particular technology has penetrated a significant portion of the market, it may be very difficult to dislodge. Fortunes in the computer industry have been made and lost from the recognition that people do not want to switch to a new piece of hardware or software—even if it is demonstrably superior—because they will lose both the time they have invested in old ways and the ability to share data easily with others. If buyers, sellers and distributors of information goods make the wrong choices now, repairing the damage could be very costly."[19]

FIVE NEOTERIC FORCES

Varian says there are five neoteric forces, or forces of recent origin, at work in the world that should be considered when making an economic analysis of new economy companies:

1. *Differentiation of products and prices:* "One of the great things about information technology is, you can do one-to-one marketing, you can do mass customization. You can also reach millions and millions at lower cost."[20] This strategy of creating different versions of the same core of information by tailoring to the needs of different customers can take an endless number of forms. Versioning strategy can help a company distinguish its products from competitors and protect its prices from collapse.

The world of outdoor sports provides an excellent example: A biking enthusiast searching for mountain bike trails by flipping on his computer and going to the Internet will find unbidden website ads popping up, for biking gear. The financial services industry often engages in versioning as well. There are multiple ways and cost levels to providing stock market information. For example, 20-minute-delayed quotes may be given away, but quicker, more sophisticated, more interactive information comes at a price. Bare-bones financial information, little more than that given in newspaper stock price charts, is free, but anything beyond that requires that an investor register with a broker or enroll for an ongoing subscription service.

2. *Rights management:* The cost of copying and distribution is suddenly vastly lower, and not just for providers, but for pirates as well. Those who create intellectual property not only have to think about the best way to protect their property rights, but also the best way to exploit them.

3. *Switching/lock-in:* Once a user makes a technology choice, he is stuck with it for a long time. His unwillingness to spend time and money switching products locks him into his first choice. The seller wants to maximize this effect; the buyer wants to minimize it.

4. *Networks and positive feedback:* Early positive feedback in high tech can be based on expectations and have both negative and positive effects. If consumers expect a product to become popular, a bandwagon forms. But if consumers expect the product to flop, the expectation of failure will become a self-fulfilling prophecy.

Once a product is on the market and gains a foothold, and the more people use a technology, the easier it is for others to use it as well. The network gets bigger and bigger. Thus, a natural advantage accrues to the leader, usually the first one to enter the market.

5. *Standardization:* The larger a network becomes, the more other products need to conform to its parameters. Thus the more valuable the network becomes. There is an enormous economic and functional advantage in interconnectivity and standardization.[21]

Varian says that despite some limitations and difficulties, cross-fertilization between scientific disciplines can be useful. Like Arthur, he sees that "Economics has, in fact, learned a lot from physics, biology and mathematics. And even when such attempts at interdisciplinary communication fail, as they often do, it is interesting to see others approach the questions that are your main business."[22]

Varian's guidelines are simpler and less radical than Arthur's. Yet Varian seems to agree with Arthur that "nothing changes about human nature, nothing really changes about some of the real basics of the economy. People still choose, more or less, what is the best course of action for themselves."[23]

VALUATIONS

With all this information in mind, Bill Miller still relies on the old-fashioned value analysis of stocks, but he does it against the backdrop of a deep and intuitive understanding of high tech.

"*We buy businesses that sell at large discounts to our assessment of their underlying value,*" *he explains.* "*So the question is, where are the best values in the market? Are they among companies that are growing, companies that are shrinking or are cyclical? We own a lot of technology stocks because we think the best relative values are in that sector.*"[24]

Recognizing that the economics of high technology seems to lend itself to market domination by a few superior companies, Miller extrapolates forward to the next point. "Look at tech—Microsoft has 90 percent of its market share; Intel has 90 percent; Cisco Systems has 80 percent. They dominate. This leads to a winner-takes-all situation in most markets." And down the road, says Miller, "the technology may change, but market positions do not." Thus, investors can make investments in well-chosen high-technology companies on a long-term basis.

Even more significant, he insists, high technology companies "are susceptible to rational valuation. They may have greater volatility, which makes them somewhat different. But it is no more difficult to analyze Dell Computers versus Alcoa or U.S. Steel."

Ultimately, says Miller, "The only way you can compare any two investments is by comparing what you pay and what you expect to get."[25]

Even with limited corporate histories and scant financial figures, Miller and his staff build a matrix of the business and project out of all of the fundamentals. Using off-the-shelf software, they feed in current numbers and trends to create pictures of the future based on various assumptions. "We try to develop a long-term model of what the business is, the dynamics of the market, and so forth. We just use a bunch of different possibilities. We use so many scenarios that one of them will surely unfold," he says.[26] Then, as the real numbers come in, Miller continually adjusts his scenarios and constantly reevaluates how the new information could affect the future.

This discussion begs another question—actually a simpler one: Is high technology appealing to Miller because in many instances start-up costs can be relatively low (and marginal costs even lower), thus allowing companies to fly lighter and faster? Though Miller admits that "companies without asset intensity get to free cash flow faster," he says that hard assets can still add a lot of value, even in the new economy. For example, says Miller, take the cable television industry, which has high fixed costs and requires a high degree of maintenance. "But that is part of the 'moat' Warren Buffett talks about. It creates a barrier to entry for competitors."[27]

Buffett recognized the value of tangible assets, Miller continues, when he "bought Executive Jet Aviation, which has huge capital investment on a continuing basis. He said to Executive Jet CEO Rich Santulli, 'you'll have all the capital you need if you can dominate this business.' It was a really good purchase. All those capital costs are recoverable."[28]

Whether it is called a franchise, a moat around a business, or a margin of safety, this is the type of factor that can be so positive that an investor could make analytical errors and the investment would still remain a good one. Miller has learned that like their old economy ancestors, good hardware, software, dot.coms, and other new economy businesses "have a rising margin of safety over time. The margin of safety is not static." The value only appears stalled, Miller points out, when a company's costs are largest. "But any company that earns more than its cost of capital is a rising value, and it has a rising margin of safety."[29]

With these principles in mind, let's look at some of the companies Miller has either invested in or considered seriously for his portfolio.

When Value Trust was established in 1982, it held 16 stocks, almost all of them New York Stock Exchange blue chips. When Miller took charge in 1991, the list of holdings had more than tripled in size and showed its first signs of becoming tech oriented. The trend toward tech was progressive in nature. In 1990, Miller owned MCI (later MCI WorldCom) as his main technology holding. By 1992, he had added GTE Corporation, Teléfonos de Mexico, Vodafone Group PLC, and Lotus Development to the list. The very next year, Lotus posted a 35 percent gain and in 1994 it increased 28.2 percent in price. It lost its luster in 1995 with a 6.7 percent decline in price and was out of the portfolio after it was acquired by IBM in 1996. In 1993, Miller placed the biotechnology company Amgen on his list. He added Nokia in 1996 and Nextel in 1999. Dell and America Online were added in 1996, Gateway in 1999, and Amazon.com in 2000.

AMGEN

Not long after Bill Clinton moved into the White House, health care stocks went into decline because of the administration's dislike for high profits in the industry and because of fears (unfounded as they were) of health care reform. Amgen also was being punished by a sales slowdown in Neupogen, a drug used to treat infection in people receiving bone-marrow-suppressing drugs for cancer treatment. Neupogen was Amgen's major product. The biotech company was trading at about $40 when Miller bought it, and would earn $3 the next year. Miller anticipated about 20 percent growth per year. "It does not raise prices on its drugs," he said, "so even drug price controls would not inhibit its growth [though other aspects of health care reform could]."[30]

Miller was not in fact overly worried about the projected reforms and expected to make more investments in beaten-down health care companies. "Reorganizing 14 percent of the GDP, which is what health care represents, is a gargantuan task and one that is highly unlikely to even begin, must less be completed, this year (1993)," he noted. "We believe meaningful legislation will not be passed before next year and that the more comprehensive the changes sought, the greater the likelihood of delay."[31]

By the 1994 annual report, Miller was no longer addressing health care reform. Attention had now turned to Amgen's earnings.

He increased his holdings when the stock's price deflated due to fears of poor earnings. The stock regained its ground when earnings were surprisingly good. "Even after the rebound, Amgen sells at only 12 times earnings with a 15 percent estimated growth rate, significant excess cash generation, and an active share buyback program."[32]

By the end of that year, Amgen was one of Miller's best performers with a 14.2 percent gain in price. The stock blew hot and cold for a few years, then in 1999 was on fire with a 146 percent return. By the end of that year, Miller had sold the stock.

AMAZON.COM

Miller's most controversial investment ever—in the on-line retailer Amazon.com—surely has given him thick skin. Critics of the investment never seem to cease. Harvey Eisen of Bedford Oak Advisors LLC, appearing with Miller on a panel, jokingly asked him if he was drunk when he decided Amazon was cheap.[33] A *Barron's* reader noted in a letter to the editor that even after the Internet stock collapse, Miller still pledged his fealty to Amazon. "Nice to have that kind of faith in a firm he apparently bought at much higher prices and has continued to like all the way down." The letter writer himself had questioned the valuation of retail dot.coms during the months when they were trading at their peak. "Well I'm no Warren Buffett. Then again, judging by his apparent gross misjudgment of Amazon, neither is Bill Miller."[34]

Another *Barron's* reader goaded Miller even deeper: "Certainly, no one this side of Alpha Centauri is surprised that Bill Miller, tending a herd of 40 million Amazon.com shares, suggests that buying Amazon is a swell idea. But where would you buy the shares? What astute shareholder, knowing that Amazon.com hails from a galaxy where 'the accounting stuff makes no difference,' could consider selling?"[35]

Never mind those jokers. Miller stuck where he was. Had he been using traditional valuation measures, Miller says he never would have taken a look at Amazon.com. However, he had developed expertise in the Internet and had been working with Dell and AOL, and over time, became acquainted with Amazon's management. This opened his eyes to the possibilities. One reason value investors shun the tech sector is that product cycles are short, business risk is high, and the companies seldom look cheap even when they're on the skids. Yet Miller found his two most successful investments, AOL and Dell, in the traditional way—following bad news or a disappointing profit report.

Miller believed that unlike other e-tailers, Amazon had sufficient capital to weather the large losses necessary to build a critical mass of customers. Customers separate winners from losers on the Internet.[36]

"What companies like Etoys need to do—and what Ameritrade and E-Trade already are doing—is spend large amounts of money to attract customers," Miller noted in 1999. "But there just aren't that many customers out there to go around."[37]

Amazon was founded by Jeffrey P. Bezos in 1995 and went public in 1997. The powerful, dominant Amazon River, with its countless branches and tributaries, is the perfect metaphor for Bezos's company. With more than 25 million customers with year 2001 sales of $3.1 billion, it is the world's biggest consumer e-commerce company. At the end of 1999, the company was worth more than $40 billion on the stock market.

Miller remained convinced that the market misunderstood Amazon. He illustrated his point at a year 2000 conference held by the newsletter *Grant's Interest Rate Observer.* After passing out a questionnaire to the attending fund managers, he asked them to guess the cumulative cash loss for Amazon since its inception. Their estimates ranged from a low of $200 million to as high as $4 billion. The correct answer—$62 million. "We don't believe that the market is correctly analyzing Amazon," Miller insisted. "I mean, these guys were pros."[38] At the time Amazon was trading at around $50, and Miller expected it to hit $90 within the year.

However, the high-flying company soon took a terrible tumble, with stocks plummeting in mid-2000 after Lehman Brothers analysts said they felt the company's credit was "extremely weak and deteriorating." By the end of 2000, its capitalization was beaten down to $9.4 billion. In hindsight, the collapse was predictable. Amazon sells everything from books to drill bits, but by 2002 had lost $3 billion. Despite heavy on-line competition from traditional retailers such as Wal-Mart, Bezos promised Amazon would have an operating profit by the end of 2001, and he kept his promise.

THE NEW RETAIL WORLD: AMAZON AND DELL

According to Miller's analysis, though Amazon is compared to other on-line retailers, it has an economic model that is more like Dell than that of the other leading bookstore chain, Barnes & Noble.[39] He argues that a new economy e-tailer such as Amazon.com makes a tiny capital expenditure, compared to its brick-and-mortar counterparts. Even more significant, Amazon collects revenues immediately when customers charge their purchases, but it doesn't need to pay suppliers for 50 days. So it is the suppliers, not the shareholders, who are funding the company's growth. The balance sheet, the working capital accounts, rather than the income statement, generates the cash. Dell Computers has used the same principle to get cash-rich. The company builds personal computers to order, collects payment immediately, slashes inventory costs, and then takes its time paying suppliers.[40]

Amazon and Dell, over the long term, have roughly the same gross margins—in the low 20 percent range (Amazon's is a little higher than Dell's); both will have an operating margin of 10 percent; they have approximately the same capital velocity, the same negative working capital, the same cash conversion cycle, and the same direct-to-customer marketing model. When Dell was at the same stage as Amazon is now, it was not losing money; in fact, it was generating a lot of free cash. "But Dell was selling $2,000 computers at a 20 percent gross margin, generating a $400 contribution to profit from the sale of a computer. Amazon is selling—and I'm oversimplifying this—$20 books at a 20 percent margin, giving a $4 contribution to profit. The actual gross profit dollars are a lot lower, but the fulfillment costs are not revenue dependent, they are unit based. The fulfillment costs will drop over time as the price per unit of the stuff they sell goes up, and that's the critical issue with Amazon."[41]

When he looks at Amazon, Miller focuses on its domestic books, videos, and music business, since this is Amazon's most mature and profitable segment. In that segment Amazon had an 8 percent operating margin at the time, and was making money. Amazon's other businesses had even better economics and were growing rapidly by the new century, with consumer electronics as its second largest sector.

"So if they sell a Palm Pilot at $400 and a 20 percent margin, that's an $80 profit contribution, and the fulfillment costs to take that out of the warehouse and ship are the same as if you were selling a book. If they can make money at the books-music-and-video level, we are quite confident they can make money in all of the other businesses."[42]

As for its foreign presence, Amazon is the number 1 on-line retailer in the United Kingdom, Germany, and Japan and number 2 in France. This is significant, since very few U.S.-based retailers operate successfully abroad. "As Jeff Bezos says—correctly—try and find a lot in downtown Tokyo to open a retail store. They [Amazon] have a tremendous model advantage in the business. A lot of things that currently cause Amazon to lose money and generate negative cash flow—software development costs and a purchasing disadvantage in consumer electronics—will be over by the end of this year, we expect. Next year [2002] we estimate the company will be cash neutral at worst. When that changeover happens, and it is clear they are not going to disappear and they are not going to dilute you with some massive offering, then the perception of the company and the underlying valuation will change significantly."[43] When Amazon reported its first profit (from the fourth quarter of 2000), the stock rallied about 40 percent.

Despite the e-tailer's sunny outlook, Bezos has had difficulty convincing most investors of the wisdom of his ways. Right after the dawn of the millennium, Amazon made a big bet in M-commerce, or Internet connection by mobile phone technology. "Amazon Anywhere" didn't work out, at least not so far, and Amazon started laying people off in that sector. Perhaps it didn't work because shopping from a mobile telephone or a handheld computer just isn't convenient. The products are difficult to see on the screen and putting in information is slow and easily messed up. Just not fun.[44] In the late summer of 2001, Amazon began selling computers on-line, which seemed to terrify investors, and the share price again declined.

The swarm of flies on Amazon's business flow, however, has been its accounting, which some describe as confusing and others say is downright misleading.[45] The problem is one discussed in Chapter 3—pro-forma accounting. In the previously mentioned May 2001 article decrying the practice of this method of calculation, *Business Week* reported, "In its April 24 results announcement, [Amazon] reported a 'pro-forma operating' loss of $49 million in the first quarter of this year. Confusingly, it also reported a 'pro-forma net' loss of 21 cents a share, or a total of $76 million. Investors had to pick carefully among a slew of numbers to see that Amazon actually had a net loss of $234 million, or 66 cents a share, using GAAP."[46] Among the missing business costs in the pro-forma report were a net interest expense of $24 million and a $114 million charge for restructuring costs, including the cost of closing a warehouse. (Amazon spokesman Bill Curry defended Amazon's numbers, saying that the GAAP reporting results were included in the report. However, he said pro-forma numbers were included as well, because that is "how we think about our business.")[47]

In terms of pro-forma accounting, Miller is willing to cut companies a little slack. He contends that just because a company follows GAAP doesn't mean the numbers reflect the underlying reality of the company.

"I'm going to dispose of the accounting very quickly. The accounting stuff makes no difference. We are interested in the underlying economic reality of the business and not how they report what is going on. I think a lot of the issues that people have raised are bogus. Go back to AOL [now AOL Time Warner] back in 1996, when we were buying

that. Everybody was concerned because they were capitalizing the cost of acquiring subscribers instead of expensing it. The costs were what they were, it didn't really matter how they were accounting for it. They were spending money to acquire subscribers. We understood the underlying principles.[48]

When Miller bought into Amazon, he recognized that it might take 10 years for the investment to reach full valuation, and recent events confirm that probability. Miller acquired his first Amazon.com stock at a price in the low-$80s, but his average overall cost for his Amazon shares is in the low $30s. Miller said that the on-line retailer is cash-flow positive now and that he expected it to remain so forever, which means it would never need access to the capital markets.[49]

In 2000, Miller swapped the stock in the Opportunity Trust for convertible bonds to obtain a tax loss on the stock and because the bonds had better risk/reward characteristics. Convertible bonds pay a coupon and can be swapped into shares of the company. Nevertheless, Legg Mason, with more than 50 million shares, owns 16 percent of the company. Legg Mason is the largest outside investor in Amazon; only Bezos earns more.

When asked in a May 2001 *Barron's* interview about his faithful interest in Amazon.com, Miller replied:

"I'm reluctant to talk about it because Alan Abelson is a national journalistic treasure and I'm afraid to send him to an early grave if I use the

> *words 'buy' and 'Amazon' in your publication*
> *contiguously. But yes, we have high conviction in*
> *Amazon. And we currently own more than 40*
> *million shares of it. We are also the largest holders*
> *as far as I can tell, of the convertible bonds."*[50]
> *How much did Miller think Amazon was worth?*
> *"A lot."*[51]

David Diamond, manager of Boston-based High Rock Asset Management, doesn't see things the way Miller does. "I like annuity-based businesses that throw off excess free cash flow. I am sure Bill Miller would make the comment that once Amazon gets to break even it's all gravy and you get big margins. But there are plenty of other companies I'd rather own."[52]

DELL VERSUS GATEWAY

Miller took advantage of the 1996 panic surrounding a feared slow-down in personal computer demand to scoop up shares of Dell. Texas-based Dell Computers is operated by 36-year-old savvy busi-nessman Michael Dell. The company's direct sales model allows ex-tremely high returns on capital compared to its competition. Thanks to Dell's clever use of the net to do everything from handling cus-tomer orders to linking suppliers during the high-tech salad days, he was selling $50 million worth of personal computers daily. When the PC market shriveled, he reduced inventories to a meager 5 days' worth, down from 12 days in 1997.

Among the lessons Miller learned from his fellow scholars and their imaginative mentors at the Santa Fe Institute is how apparent competitors, be they birds or chip manufacturers, can coexist and thrive, and nowhere was this more apparent than in the case of Dell and a similar company, Gateway, in the mid to late 1990s.[53]

Late in 1998, Miller also acquired a stake in Gateway, buying in the $50-per-share range. Within 6 months, the shares had risen to $70, and Miller expected the price to go as high as $90. Gateway's price-to-earnings multiple was 17 times the 1999 forecast (compared to Dell's 58 at the time), which seemed to give Gateway plenty of room for growth.[54]

Even though Gateway appeared to be Dell's poor relation, Miller says this was a common misunderstanding. The two companies then had strengths in different markets: "Dell [is] in the large corporate segment, Gateway in the consumer segment. Dell's success, e.g., is coming at the expense of Compaq and Hewlett-Packard, not Gateway."[55] The distinction between Dell and Gateway's market positions has become less clear cut in recent years. Dell now has a larger position in the consumer market and Gateway has entered the corporate segment. By early 2002, Dell's substantially higher and growing market share and much lower cost position had significantly eroded Gateway's ability to coexist.

Even so, Miller contends that back then many value investors misunderstood Dell. He bought the company when it traded at less than 5 times the next year's expected earnings. "If you look at historical valuations of personal-computer stocks, their prices used to bounce between six and 12 times earnings. When Dell fell to a P/E of six, value investors moved in. When it rose to 12, investors sold."[56]

But not Miller.

"Because we analyze businesses, not historic stock-trading patterns, I was surprised to find that Dell was worth four times what we paid for it—that is, when we bought it for $2, adjusted for subsequent stock splits, I figured its real value at $8, based on our analysis of free cash flow and other factors, including a return on capital of 35 percent. Since then, the company's revenue growth has far exceeded what we projected. And return on capital rose in 18 months from 35 percent to 229 percent—the highest in American industry. Now if it was worth four times the $2 we paid, and subsequently became seven times more profitable, you can understand why we kept raising the value of the company. We estimate its value in the low to mid $80s, versus its current price of $75."[57]

AOL TIME WARNER

Miller was an early investor in one of the Internet's most striking companies: America Online Inc. Steve Case, AOL's founder and chief executive officer, brought the Internet (and especially e-mail) to 29 million people via a Simple Simon service. From his discussions at the Santa Fe Institute, Miller came to understand that "once AOL's network had reached 50 percent of the share of the market for on-line customers, they had created an entity that is impregnable." As strong as Microsoft is, it has not been able to put AOL out of business. "It would be difficult for anyone to knock AOL off."[58]

Lisa Rapuano had a big influence on the AOL analysis. She believed that Wall Street misunderstood the significance of AOL's problems. The Internet access provider was the subject of a lot of criticism because it had not been able to quickly satisfy the demands of a rush of new customers. Rapuano figured that the higher demand only meant that people were buying into the concept—customers loved the service. She persuaded Miller to buy a million shares.[59]

Her analysis was right on the mark. AOL now dominates the consumer on-line access market. With the astounding acquisition of Time Warner, Steve Case was the mastermind of the most powerful combination of old and new media. At the time it happened, AOL Time Warner was the biggest merger in U.S. history at $97 billion (it started out even bigger but was adjusted down as the market reacted to the news). The deal seemed confounding, considering the inflated price of AOL and the solid assets of Time Warner. AOL's price was strong until the merger was announced on January 10, 2000. But later, even with the Internet crash, most analysts believed that Time Warner shareholders got more than their money's worth in the deal. Miller continued to have a positive outlook, though he did reduce his position slightly. Miller acquired $1 million shares of AOL in November of 1996, and those shares split four times between 1998 and 1999, giving the funds $116 million shares in all. The cost adjusted basis for the AOL shares is $1.625 per share. In December 1997 Miller bought 362,500 more shares, which have a cost basis of $5.964. "We made 50 times our money," says Miller.[60] The value of

121

the AOL shares at the end of 2001 was around $600 million, making it one of Miller's largest holdings, although the value was down from its peak value of more than $2 billion.

As was the case with Amazon.com, AOL's accounting presents a challenge to analysts. Miller may have understood the reporting standards used by AOL, but not everyone appreciated them, including the SEC, which eventually took action against the company. For years, AOL deferred the marketing expense of sending out millions of computer disks to anyone and everyone who seemed like a potential customer. Deferring that cost made AOL appear more profitable than it actually was. This led to issuing more securities for cash and acquisitions that fed its growth. On May 15, 2000, AOL reached a settlement with the SEC. Without admitting or denying any wrongdoing, AOL paid a $3.5 million fine and restated its former income as loss. By then, the give-away ploy had locked in the market and AOL was home free as an Internet giant.

"If AOL were by itself today, its stock price would be a lot lower," claimed David W. Tice, a money manager who publishes the earnings watch bulletin *Behind the Numbers.* And yet, the accounting aggressiveness achieved AOL's long-term goal.[61]

Nevertheless, Morningstar CEO Don Phillips and others defended Miller's interest in stocks such as AOL. "Just as Buffett moved beyond the Ben Graham asset valuation models that worked for steel companies to pioneer methods that could value companies with more nebulous franchise value like media companies, so too are we starting to see managers like Bill Miller developing a valuation for tech," he said.[62]

One of the reasons Miller did well with AOL was because he built extra safety into his calculations. Again, when a company is growing as rapidly as AOL, Miller gives himself some wiggle room in the evaluation buy using an unusually high discount rate—30 percent. That's about three times what he would use on IBM, and it provides a margin of safety that is a critical part of the value discipline. Miller first started buying the stock in 1996. Adjusted for splits, his cost for AOL is $3 per share. By 1999, Miller's shares had risen 750 percent.[63]

At its peak, AOL represented 15 percent of Value Trust's total worth.[64] When the AOL–Time Warner merger was completed in early 2001, Miller's Value Trust ended up with 5.66 percent of its portfolio in the stock.

Miller believes that the combined AOL–Time Warner has competitive advantages. It has the largest and best collection of assets in an industry where media is connected to high tech. It has interactive assets including a powerful mix of content and distribution. "As a business, it will be around for a long time and it will be valuable," Miller predicts.[65]

NEXTEL

Miller carried telecommunication stocks in his portfolio for years, and overall did well with them. In 1999, he began buying Nextel, a wireless telephone company with a global network. By the end of 2000, he had sold almost all of these shares in the $60s, repurchasing millions more at $15 and lower as interest in telecom stocks evaporated in 2001. Nextel was already getting hammered, but the situation got worse following the September 11 terrorist attacks. The price plummeted to around $9 per share, and rather than be alarmed, Miller saw the opportunity to strengthen his position. He acquired an additional half million shares, bringing his stake in the company to around $400 million. Nextel was attractive to Miller because it has the highest average revenue per unit in the industry. Its Nextel Direct Connect differentiates the company from Sprint PCs, AT&T Wireless, and other competitors.

To evaluate this particular business, Miller broke it into segments. The domestic business, he pointed out, was trading at around 10 times enterprise value to estimated earnings before interest, taxes, depreciation, and amortization (EBITDA). EBITDA was expected to grow about 70 percent in 2001 and 50 percent the following year, representing a very rapid growth of cash stream. The stock traded at 7.5 times enterprise value to estimated EBITDA in 2002 and five times in 2003. Miller figured that would mean, at a minimum, $30 per share.[66]

SYMANTEC

Symantec is an emerging company in the Internet security business. It is run by former IBM-er John Thompson and sells antivirus programs under its Norton brand. Miller expects to see top-line growth of about 25 percent a year, and generation of $50 million free cash flow each quarter, with $10 per share in cash. It should be buying back shares, and trades at less than 15 times next year's earnings. As Miller sees it, "We can't find any company that has a better position in a very powerful, important market with really good management, that has faster top-line growth and a lower multiple, better cash generation and a superior balance sheet with 10 bucks a share in cash."[67] Miller's analysis paid off, but for an unexpected reason. Between the end of September, 2001 and the end of the year, due to fears of further terrorist attacks, business boomed and the stock price soared more than 90 percent.

MICROSOFT

This is a could-have, would-have, should-have analysis. In 1999, Miller said that if he had understood valuation better, he would have owned Microsoft and Cisco Systems. In general, he noted, stocks are not undervalued just because they go up over some short time frame. "But it's hard to make a case that they are not undervalued if they go up year after year over long periods of time—especially when they've provided excess rates of return over the market."[68]

Quantitative analyst Edward Keon, of Prudential Securities Inc., did a Miller-type investigation of Microsoft. Keon says that investment managers now, at least, are willing to do some "outside-the-box" thinking about securities such as Microsoft. Here's how Keon saw the situation with Microsoft back in 1999.

First, he examined the quality of the earnings. About 67 percent of Microsoft's profits came from sales that were booked in the same quarter, versus 38.9 percent for the median company in the S&P. It's virtually as if two-thirds of the profits had come from cold cash, which is good, because with receivables there's always a risk that the company may not get paid.

To put the average S&P-listed company on a par with Microsoft, Keon adjusts the total S&P earnings for the cash factor. In this late 1999 scenario, the S&P forecasted earnings dropped from $54 to about $31, which raised its P/E to nearly 42 from 24. Using that measure, Microsoft, with a P/E of 52, was not that much more expensive than the average stock. "The real gap between Microsoft's valuation and the market's valuation may not be as wide as the raw numbers indicate," said Keon.[69]

Keon also looks at the growth rate of earnings. Microsoft profits grew at about 40 percent a year during the previous 5 years (1994 to 1999), he said, and it is expected that the company will grow at about 24 percent per year until about 2004. The S&P earnings grew only at a rate of 10 percent over the previous 5 years, and were forecast to grow only 15 percent during the next 5. This means Microsoft's P/E is 2.2 times its estimated earnings growth rate, while the S&P 500's cash-adjusted P/E is 2.8 times the forecasted earnings growth rate. Keon interpreted this to mean that Microsoft was cheaper than the average company, and to him this made it a value stock.[70]

THE TECH IMPLOSION

By anyone's measure, the 1990s were a strange era for business—and especially for high tech and the emerging Internet segment. In the last 4 years of the decade, the S&P 500 gained about 26 percent per year compounded, while the tech-laden Nasdaq gained more than 40 percent. Somehow it seemed that the more money a company lost, the better its stock fared, and the more it earned, the worse the share performed. Amazon, iVillage, and Priceline all took pride in the cash they were burning, ostensibly to "buy eyeballs," or build a customer base for their sites.

Throughout the decade there was another curious development: Although the economy was strong in the 1990s, companies were unable to raise prices, and inflation stayed low. But then, the lower prices meant flatter profits.

Miller began worrying in early 2000 that the tech market might implode, and on March 10 of that year he became convinced: "Nasdaq was up 24 percent for the year, the Dow was down 13 percent. Over a 12-month period, Nasdaq was up 112 percent and the Dow was down 3. It struck me that these figures were just unbelievable. Emotionally extreme. Tech valuations were clearly at idiotic levels."[71]

He saw another danger sign. In the first quarter of 2000, 66 percent of fund managers outperformed the S&P. Yet the only two sectors that beat the index over that time were technology and utilities. "Fund managers were following a very simple-minded rule: You overweight tech, you outperform. It was an indication to me that we were nearing the end."[72]

In Miller's view, the stampede to tech was exacerbated in part by value-oriented money managers who felt pressure to buy tech stocks, their better sense be damned. Several fund managers had been fired because of their reluctance to be heavily weighted in tech, and Julian Robertson's $20 billion Tiger Management dissolved that year because of poor performance as a result of his preference for old-economy stocks. The *New York Times* declared the demise of Tiger as the death of value as a viable principle. The *Times* headline read "The End of the Game."

This last event waved a red flag in Miller's direction. He'd been worried about the market before, but now he reduced his exposure from 39 percent of the fund to 26 percent. "We were overweight in tech, now we're underweight. We're back to the old technology stocks, the traditional staple of most value investors."[73]

Indeed, the deluge came, and it came quickly. The tech-dominated Nasdaq topped out at 5049 on March 10, 2000. One month later, the Nasdaq was down 14 percent for the year and down 31 percent from its March 10 summit. The Dow was down 7 percent for the year, but was up 10 percent, including dividends from March 10. Most stocks had been declining for 2 years, but the retreat was masked by the aggressive advance in large capitalization growth and technology shares.

By the start of 2001, widely held tech leaders Microsoft, Lucent, Motorola, and Intel were off an average of 60 percent from the year's high. Internet stocks took an especially brutal beating, which murdered off many and left others barely clinging to life. Yahoo and e-Bay, among the best of the sector, ended the year 2000 off an average of 79 percent. As of October 10, 2001, Yahoo was trading at $10.87 and e-Bay was trading at $55.63.

SHIFTING TIDES

In the final years of the technology stock boom, equity investors took on the role of financing fledgling companies early in their development—a role traditionally handled by venture capitalists. Prior to that time, companies could not go public without a track record that proved their ability to turn a profit.

Consequently, in the first quarter of 2000, fewer than one in five companies that made initial public stock offerings had profitable operations. In 1995, almost two-thirds of new issuers were profitable when they went public.[74]

Between the spring of 2000 and 2001, investors lost almost $4 trillion in market value. What went wrong in the market decline of 2000? In April 2000, just about the time he spoke to Mauboussin's class at Columbia, Miller announced on the Legg Mason web site that he believed that there was a major strategic shift underway in the stock market, the first such shift in 4 or 5 years. It was a shift away from technology stocks back to nontechnology issues. He said that much of the excessive returns that his shareholders had enjoyed in the past 4 to 5 years had been because he'd been able to buy shares of first-rate technology companies before they were recognized by the market. But that atmosphere had dissolved, and now most investors were crowded into technology companies.

"There has been a tremendous public belief in technology stocks coupled with a tremendous professional belief in these stocks as the way to out-perform. And as typically happens when everyone figures out what the game is, the game changes," explained Miller.

The danger signs in the market included the high amount of capitalization in technology (out of proportion to the sector's influence on the economy perhaps?) and increased volatility in the market. Miller also noted that the NASDAQ had outperformed the Dow and the S&P 500 for 2 years in a row and that he had never seen that happen 3 years running. He went on to emphasize that he was not antitechnology, but simply that he believed valuations were out of whack. He noted that the P/E ratios of companies in the market (those with earnings) peaked in 1998 at 19.7 times. After 1998, P/Es began to decline, meaning that near-term growth in P/Es in general was suspect. He called this a "multiple burn-off." Miller added that the correction would take a relatively long time to play out because "It's very difficult for people to give up beliefs that are held with the kind of tenacity that the technology boom has elicited."[75]

Another reason tech investors may have held on too long is because they did not read balance sheets on many high-flying high-tech stocks. Therefore, they missed such warning signs as bloated inventories and rising accounts receivable. These warning signs appeared in the financial documents of such companies as Cisco Systems, Nortel Networks, Alcatel, and Gateway.

"*The value of any investment is the present value of the future free cash flows that it will generate for its owners,*" *wrote Miller to his shareholders in 2001. "Therefore, the market prices a company's stock based on future earnings expectations which are discounted by a forecasted growth rate to arrive at a present value. If estimates of future profitability are lowered, then the stock price declines. As sales surged in the technology and telecommunications sectors in the late 1990s so did future growth expectations, which in turn sent these stock prices soaring. A confluence of extraordinary factors, including massive expenditures for Y2K readiness, were responsible for the astonishing growth during the period. As these extraordinary factors faded, so did overly optimistic expectations for future profits."[76]*

"In the meantime," Miller reported, "the same relatively small number of stocks that propelled major market indexes higher in the late 1990s caused the sharp declines over the past year when investors finally scrutinized their lofty valuations. Nevertheless over the past year the average stock performed better than it did during the technology bull market of the late 1990s. Indeed, a stealth bear market in the broader market was present between 1997 and 2000, but was masked by surging prices in the technology and telecommunications sectors."[77]

Following the 2000–2001 stock market crash, Bill Fleckenstein, a money manager at Fleckenstein Capital in Seattle, made the point that traditional measures of value still have merit. "There ought to be a law in this country that before you're allowed to buy a stock you have to be able to read its balance sheet. That's where companies try to hide everything. That's where all the shenanigans show up."[78] Allan Sloan, Wall Street editor of *Newsweek* magazine, urged his fellow journalists to start covering tech companies the way they would any other corporation. In addition to examining earnings reports, financial writers should study cash flow and particularly how much of that cash represents borrowed money.[79]

HAS HIGH TECH BEEN BROUGHT TO HEEL?

George Gilder, a man who thinks a lot about technology, has said, "The central event of the twentieth century is the overthrow of matter. In technology, economics, and the politics of nations, wealth in the form of physical resources is steadily declining in value and significance. The powers of mind are everywhere ascendant over the brute force of things."[80]

In a similar vein, in the wake of the Internet washout, Hal Varian has taken it upon himself to convince the establishment business world that the bursting of the Internet bubble doesn't mean they can ignore the revolution the Internet hath wrought. The advent of the Internet remains transformational. To understand that a future remains for high tech, an investor need look no further than the stock markets themselves.

"Before the telegraph," wrote Varian, "the U.S. had some 50 stock exchanges; afterwards, it had essentially one. Before the Internet there were dozens of international financial markets. How many will survive by 2010? Last week's announcement of the merger of the London and Frankfurt markets is the latest sign of a wave of financial market consolidation. Everyone in the industry recognizes that there will be fewer stock markets in the future and that the survivors will be primarily electronic exchanges.

"The markets themselves have been forecasting the demise of floor trading: despite record volumes, the value of seats on the New York Stock Exchange, the Chicago Board of Trade and the Chicago Mercantile Exchange has fallen by 30 percent to 60 percent in the last five years.

"In terms of providing liquidity, bigger markets are better. But the more trades there are, the more complex the market becomes. Modern markets couldn't exist without information technology support in the back office that manages this complexity. But now, in a palace revolt, the back office is taking over the trading floor.

"When given the choice, investors prefer the speed and convenience of electronic execution. The Paris futures exchange, Matif, is a case in point. When it introduced electronic trading, it kept floor trading, assuming the market would eventually decide which was superior. 'Eventually' came a lot sooner than anyone expected. Within two weeks nearly everyone was trading electronically; within eight weeks, Matif closed floor trading entirely due to lack of demand."[81]

When things settle down, Varian claims, new technology will be as powerful as everyone expected, but just in different ways than they thought. Technology remains very much with us, and the words of J.R.R. Tolkien apply: "It does not do you good to leave a dragon out of your calculations if you live near him."

CHAPTER *6*

HIGH TECH AND REGULATION IN BRIEF

Hey Yogi, I think we're lost.　　　　　　　　—Phil Rizzuto

Yeah, but we're making great time.　　　　　—Yogi Berra

Antitrust—government keeping the brakes on big business—is one of those issues in American culture that can set friend against friend and brother against brother. It is as complex as it is confusing and divisive. Americans didn't like seeing John D. Rockefeller's oil empire broken up in the 1920s and bristled at the dismantling of American Telephone and Telegraph in the 1980s. Even though the split-off Standard Oils and the Baby Bells went right on to grow and prosper, trust busting goes against the American grain. Prosecuting copyright and patent infringement is a little easier for people to swallow, but in a country that treasures free speech even this remains suspect. Just look at how often McDonald's has to protect its brand name by legal measures. Yet despite public bias, the Justice Department has always been suspicious of illegal practices in emerging technologies, and often with good cause.

The justification and effectiveness of government measures are always up for debate, especially among investors, who harbor a deep dislike for any sort of uncertainty. The 1970s case against IBM was abandoned at the instruction of Ronald Reagan when he was elected president. Despite that company's fortunate break, market forces—

the emergence of Microsoft Corp. in particular—brought IBM to heel. In the 1990s, the Justice Department turned its antitrust guns on high tech again. While Justice looked at various companies, Microsoft became the main target. When George W. Bush took office in 2001, some of the heat (although not all) was diverted from Microsoft. But for many investors, the question remains: Are high-tech companies perpetually at risk for antitrust and other legal action?

A GAME THAT MAKES ITS OWN RULES

Perhaps so. Massachusetts Institute of Technology's Paul Krugman seems to think that the industry creates an antitrust atmosphere by way of its own behavior. "Information technology is no longer something idealists do for fun; not only has it become big business, it has also become a business whose underlying rules practically invite antisocial practices like price discrimination and predation. In short, say goodbye to the geeks in their garages, and say hello to the new railroad barons—and by the way, see you in court."[1]

TIME TO BUNT

Yet even Brian Arthur (whose writing and research helped revive antitrust economics, and as explained in Chapter 2, were used in the Justice Department's case against Microsoft) admits that he has mixed feelings about the campaign against Microsoft and other high-tech companies. "The wrong type of regulation could turn the high-tech sector into something like the high-tech sector in Europe or Japan," he notes, "not the wild and wonderful free-for-all that it is now. I think America has an absolutely wonderful record of innovation in high technology, and I would hate to see that hampered."[2]

Hal R. Varian says the legal problems involved here extend beyond antitrust issues. Copyright, patents, and other protections for creative work are at risk: "If intellectual property protection is too lax, there may be inadequate incentives to produce new electronic works; conversely, if protection is too strict, it may impede the free flow and fair use of information. A compromise position must be found somewhere between those who suggest that all information should be free and those who advocate laws against the electronic equivalent of browsing at a magazine rack."[3]

"I believe," Varian continues, "that extending existing copyright and patent law to apply to digital technologies can only be a stopgap measure. Law appropriate for the paper-based technology of the 18th century will not be adequate to cope with the digital technology of the 21st century; already the proliferation of litigation over software patents and even over the shape of computer-screen trash cans makes the need for wholesale revisions apparent."[4]

TELEGRAPH, TELEPHONE, THE INTERNET

The entire issue of high-tech regulation and antitrust law circulates around the evolving economics. Some would claim that the Internet is nothing more than another version, although definitely a more advanced incarnation, of the telephone. This suggests to economist/author Carl Shapiro that the government should be more rather than less diligent about antitrust and other regulations.

Shapiro helped lead the Justice Department's investigation of Microsoft from 1995 to 1996 and advised Intel Corp. in its defense against the Federal Trade Commission. Shapiro says a durable high-tech monopoly is a rare beast: "Antitrust authorities should forebear from pursuing companies that temporarily obtain market dominance based on innovation. Even a company that manages to maintain market leadership for a number of years has nothing to fear if it wins by competing on the merits. The danger area for high-tech leaders is reached when they employ business strategies that exclude rivals by impeding their ability to reach and deal with customers or complementors. Microsoft stands accused of using such exclusionary contracts with OEMs (original equipment manufacturers) and ISPs (Internet Service Providers). Smaller companies that dominate a niche can be sued for such practices, too, but most high-tech firms have nothing to fear so long as they steer clear of exclusionary practices."[5]

Shapiro writes that the current law most likely is sufficient to deal with fundamental shifts in economic markets. "The Sherman Anti-Trust Act was passed in 1890 to control monopolies. As we enter a new century, we believe it is still flexible enough to maintain the critical balance between preventing monopolization from stifling innovation, while also keeping markets competitive enough to prevent government regulation from intruding in our dynamic information-driven markets."[6]

BUTTONS AND THREADS

For Brian Arthur, it is the visual image of buttons and threads discussed in Chapter 2 that makes the computer and software industry unique and ultimately difficult to regulate. "High tech is not a commodity industry," he says. "Dominance may not so much consist in cornering a single product as in successively taking over more and more threads of the web of technology, and thereby preventing other players from getting access to new, breaking markets. It would be difficult to separate out each thread and to regulate it. And of course it may be impracticable to regulate a market before it forms—before it is fully defined."[7]

Arthur says there are no simple answers. The increasing returns situation creates even more than the normal confusion surrounding legalities and monopolies. Consider the pros and cons of operating in an economy of increasing returns:

Pro: Lock-in creates a single standard of convenience. If a product locks in because it is superior, this is fair, and it would be foolish to penalize success.

Con: A lock-in product may obstruct technological advancement. To lock in, a product usually has been discounted (or given away virtually free of charge), and this established low price is often hard to raise later.[8]

"Economies have bifurcated into two worlds—intertwined, overlapping, and different," Arthur explains. "These two worlds operate under different economic principles. Planning, control, and hierarchy characterize [economist Alfred] Marshall's world. It is a world of materials, of processing of optimization. The increasing returns world is characterized by observation, positioning, flattened organizations, missions, teams, and cunning. It is a world of psychology, of cognition, of adaptation."[9] In other words, the high-tech climate, ever more so than the old economy, invites the unexpected, sudden change and challenge.

Thus, Arthur points out, "lock-in is not forever. Technology comes in waves, and a lock-in, such as DOS's (Direct Operating System), can only last as long as a particular wave lasts."[10]

"Short term monopolization of an increasing returns market is correctly perceived as a reward or prize for innovation and risk taking," he notes. "There is a temptation to single out dominant players and hit them with an antitrust suit. This reduces regulation to something like a brawl in an old-West saloon—if you see a head, hit it."[11]

However, Arthur says that when a new market opens up, such as electronic consumer banking, companies that already dominate standards, operating systems, and neighboring technologies should not be allowed a 10-mile start in the land rush that follows. All competitors should have equal advantage.[12]

Miller has his own take on the regulation issue. He believes that while government should be vigilant for egregious abuses of corporate power, it isn't smart to spend a lot of time and money trying to solve a problem that time will resolve itself.

NO HARM, NO FOUL

In concluding his analysis of the antitrust issue, Arthur settles on two key principles: Don't penalize success and don't give a head start to the privileged.

"The wonderful, wild spirit of innovation in America needs to have free rein," he concludes. "Let us adopt government regulations that do not penalize innovation. But let us keep these horse races fair."[13]

CHAPTER 7

OLD-ECONOMY VALUATION

I want to thank all those who made this night necessary.

Yogi Berra

Throughout Bill Miller's career, constant vigilance to the economy and to the securities markets kept him well supplied with old-economy investment ideas. In the mid-1990s, even as he expanded into high technology, Value Trust gobbled up shares of health care companies that were trampled down by concerns over President Clinton's health care plan. As noted in Chapter 4, in 1996, when Las Vegas was changing its focus from adult to family tourism and was bursting out all over with construction of big new hotels, Miller bought Circus Circus casino stock. Nevada resort hotel stocks were depressed because of the cost of new construction. Even though Circus Circus's shares had fallen from the mid-$30s to around $12, Miller continued to buy for 3 more years. He gradually quadrupled his holdings to more than 5 million shares, a position representing over 5 percent of the company. He also added Mirage Resorts and MGM Grand to his holdings. "The stocks [were] flat, but the cash flows of gaming companies have been growing," Miller insisted.[1]

In his 1996 annual report, Miller reminded Legg Mason Value Trust shareholders that he would be making what seemed like contrarian choices. The process worked this way: "We are patient, long-term investors who try to invest in solid businesses at bargain prices.

This will often lead us to being out of fashion with the market, investing where the press or public have near-term worries."[2]

COMPANIES IN A SPLIT ECONOMY

In most cases, Miller is able to apply standard business principles and traditional thinking to his old-economy investments. However, there are some economic notions that bleed from the old economy to the new, and back again. The principle of diminishing returns, for example, still grips the traditional part of the economy—the commodity and processing industries. Increasing returns, on the other hand, hold sway in the new economy—the knowledge-based industries. The situation of increasing returns can coexist with the old-economy condition of diminishing returns in some industries. So, as discussed in Chapter 2, contemporary economics is bifurcated—increasing returns and decreasing returns intertwined. It is confusing when this happens, since the old and new economies have different characteristics, behavior patterns, styles, and cultures. The two different situations frequently call for different management techniques, strategies, and attitudes about government regulation.[3]

These old-economy and new-economy companies (or parts of companies) have to be run differently. In the old economy, "Because bulk processing is repetitive, it allows constant improvement, constant optimization," explains Brian Arthur. This results in a highly structured world that allows optimization of processes.[4]

We're learning that the distinction between high- and low-tech economics is not a tidy one. Hewlett-Packard is a good example of a company that operates in both realms. The company designs knowledge-based devices in California and manufactures them in mass in other more distant locations such as Oregon and Colorado. A number of high-tech companies, or those perceived as high tech, are similarly dual-economy companies. The companies are both low- and high-tech, depending on the segment of the operation and what it does.

Service industries, such as insurance companies, restaurants, and banks, are also hybrid. Certainly the great service franchises succeed because of increasing returns, although to some extent they are affected by diminishing returns. The more McDonald's there are, for example, or the more Motel 6's there are, the better they are known and the more customers the chains attract. The increasing returns traits of service industries are on the rise, thanks to the introduction of high-tech tools. "For example," explains Arthur, "when Internet-based retail banking arrives, regional demand limitations will vanish. Each virtual bank will gain in advantage as its network increases. Barring regulation, consumer banking will then became a contest among a few large banking networks. It will become an increasing returns business. Services belong to both the processing and the increasing returns world. But their center of gravity is crossing over to the latter."[5]

BACK TO CONVENTIONAL VALUE

Miller had these principles fixed in his mind when he realized that tech values had reached an extreme level on April 4, 2000. Miller knew that the market excesses were a warning sign, and, as noted in Chapter 5, took action. "We've reached a period where valuation will begin to matter again, so we have begun reducing our technology weighting."[6]

By midsummer 2000, Miller felt sure that the market's realignment to traditional value had been confirmed. "At the beginning of 2000 we recognized that most of the under-valuation we had identified in the tech stocks we owned had been fully reflected in their share price," said Miller. "At the same time, the market was severely marking down the shares of banks and other financials. We began selling our tech names and moving the proceeds into financial and other selected names where we saw a large discrepancy between our estimate of intrinsic business value and where the shares were trading in the market."[7]

There would be consequences to the shift in focus, but there also would be some element of safety. "The rates of return [for traditional value plays] might be lower than they have been in tech," Miller said, "but there is no doubt that relative outperformance will be with value."[8]

The following charts showing the best performers and worst performers for 1999, 2000, and 2001 give some idea of how Miller's portfolio changed during those years. Additionally, by comparing year to year, it becomes clear that the worst performers quite often move to the top performers list within a very short time. The full list of Value Trust holdings for selected years are included in Appendix 1.

Value Trust—Year Ended March 31, 1999

Best Performers for Year Ended March 31, 1999

America Online, Inc.	+754.9 %
Nokia Oyj	+188.6 %
Amgen Inc.	+ 146.0 %
Dell Computer Corporation	+141.3 %
MCI WorldCom, Inc.	+ 105.7 %
International Business Machines	+ 70.6 %
Danaher Corporation	+ 37.6 %
The Kroger Co.	+ 29.6 %
General Motors Corp.	+ 28.8 %
Zion Bancorporation	+ 26.4 %

Weak Performers for Year Ended March 31, 1999

Foundation Health Systems Inc.	−55.8 %
Western Digital Corporation	−54.8 %
Starwood Hotels & Resorts Worldwide, Inc.	−46.5 %
Conseco, Inc.	−45.5 %
Metro-Goldwyn-Mayer, Inc.	−41.3 %
Toys "R" Us, Inc.	−37.4 %
Hilton Hotels Corporation	−33.8 %
Storage Technology Corporation	−26.7 %
MBIA, Inc.	−25.2 %
BankBoston Corporation	−21.4 %

Value Trust—Year Ended March 31, 2000

Best Performers for Year Ended March 31, 2000

Nextel Communications, Inc.	+304.8%
Nokia Oyj	+179.0%
Teléfonos de Mexico S.A. ADR	+103.0%
Koninklijke (Royal) Philips Electronics N.V.	+101.2%
WPP Group plc	+100.2%
Metro-Goldwyn-Mayer, Inc.	+93.8%
Gateway, Inc.	+54.6%
MGM Grand, Inc.	+42.8%
Citogroup Inc.	+39.3%
International Business Machines Corporation	+33.1%

Weak Performers for Year Ended March 31, 2000

Storage Technology Corporation	–42.8%
The Kroger Co.	–41.3%
Bank One Corporation	–37.6%
Washington Mutual, Inc.	–35.2%
Foundation Health Systems, Inc.	–34.4%
Lloyds TSB Group plc	–30.1%
Bank of America Corporation	–25.8%
MCI WorldCom, Inc.	–23.3%
Freddie Mac	–22.6%
Toys "R" Us, Inc.	–21.3%

A PAINFUL EXPERIENCE

The tech junkie on Miller's team, former Motley Fool web master Randy Befumo, didn't necessarily like the return to traditional deep value that Miller took at the end of the century. It went against all the 29-year-old knew about investing. "Yuck," he groaned. "Unum Provident, Tricon, Tupperware? These are all horrible companies. But who knows? Someday they might be really

---

Value Trust—Year Ended March 31, 2001

Best Performers for Year Ended March 31, 2001

Health Net Inc.	+157.6 %
Washington Mutual, Inc.	+106.6 %
UnitedHealth Group Incorporated	+98.8 %
Waste Management Inc.	+80.5 %
Toys "R" Us, Inc.	+69.6 %
MGIC Investment Corporation	+56.8 %
The Kroger Co.	+46.8 %
Fannie Mae	+41.0 %
MBNA Corporation	+29.8 %
Starwood Hotels & Resorts Worldwide, Inc.	+29.6 %

Weak Performers for Year Ended March 31, 2001

Amazon.com, Inc.	−84.7 %
Nextel Communications Inc.	−80.6 %
Gateway, Inc.	−68.3 %
Dell Computer Corporation	−52.4 %
AOL Time Warner Inc.	−40.3 %
WPP Group plc.	−38.9 %
General Motors Corporation	−37.4 %
Metro-Goldwyn-Mayer, Inc.	−32.6 %
Storage Technology Corporation	−31.7 %
Teléfonos de Mexico SA de CV Telmex	−23.1 %

---

good." (Unum Provident was acquired for Special Investment Trust and Tupperware for Total Return Trust.)

Even though Miller survived the tech decline better than most money managers, the experience was not painless. The fund, like its counterparts, was shaken by the turn against technology stocks, but Miller had several advantages. For one thing, he was conversant with adversity: "We had a period in the late 1980s where we underper-

---

Value Trust's Top 10 Holdings, June 30, 2001
(in order of size)

1. Waste Management Inc.
2. AOL Time Warner Inc.
3. UnitedHealth Group Inc.
4. Washington Mutual Inc.
5. MGIC Investment Corporation
6. Albertson's Inc.
7. Citigroup Inc.
8. Eastman Kodak Company
9. Bank One Corporation
10. Fannie Mae

---

formed four out of five years. And the rating on Value Trust from Morningstar and other rating services was absolutely at the bottom. People were told to avoid the fund when it was about to begin its greatest run."[9]

A FAMILIAR PATH

When Miller changed the emphasis in his portfolio from high tech to old tech, some observers realized he was following an established pattern. "Based on its performance, you could view the Legg Mason fund as sort of a time machine," said *MSN Money* writer Timothy Middleton. "It owns a bunch of names that everybody used to hate, but which have withstood the test of time. It also owns a bunch the market hates now. Its success with the former group inspires confidence that it is outsmarting the market all over again."[10]

In fact, Miller would be revisiting a sector that produced some of the best returns when he and Ernie Kiehne were working as co-managers of Value Trust.

VALUATIONS

In 2000, an interesting occurrence drew Miller's attention to under-valued financial stocks. The 1-year Treasury bill rates dipped to 4.8 percent—a number that would approximate where 3-month Treasury bill rates would be in 12 months. A short-term rate of less than 5 percent would represent a considerable decline in interest rates. If that were to occur, spreads between the cost of money and the rates charged by the bank would widen, credit quality concerns would dissipate, and loan growth would move higher. The prices of financial stocks would soar.

This would be good news in an industry that had been pelted, pounded, and pummeled by the Russian partial debt default, which in turn provoked a crash in emerging markets and sparked fears that big banks would have to write off billions in bad loans. A similar scenario had occurred in the early 1990s and twice-bitten investors were understandably skittish. The Chase Manhattan Corp. was one of Miller's larger holdings, and after Chase merged with J. P. Morgan in 2000 to become J. P. Morgan Chase & Co., Value Trust had 3.11 percent of its shares in the merged organization. By mid-2001, Washington Mutual, the nation's largest thrift, Bank One Corporation, and Fannie Mae were listed among Value Trust's top 10 holdings.

Interest rates did subside as Miller expected. By mid-2001, the 3-month Treasury bill was at 3 percent, and by the end of September, after the terrorist attack on the United States, the rate was 2.6 percent.

WASHINGTON MUTUAL

Some investors grew circumspect of Washington Mutual, a Seattle-based financial services company, in the late 1990s, primarily because of its takeover of H.F. Ahmanson & Co., another West Coast financial services company. Adding to their concerns was a flat interest rate curve that squeezed profits and Boeing's layoff of 48,000 workers in Washington State, the bank's primary market. The result was a crisis of confidence in Washington Mutual's share price. Miller began acquiring the stock in the fourth quarter of 1998.

"There are questions about how quickly the integration [of Ahmanson] will unfold and how quickly the expense cuts will take effect," noted Miller. "For people with short-term horizons, there are issues."[11]

As Miller anticipated, the immediate outlook for Washington Mutual was not glittering. With a decline of 35.2 percent, it was among the weakest performers among Value Trust's 1999–2000 securities.

Although the general consensus among analysts and investors was negative, Miller believed that Washington Mutual was poised to grow 12 percent annually in the next few years. With high-quality aggressive management running the company and a P/E of 11, the deal looked too good to pass up. It met Miller's qualifications for a traditional value buy. Indeed, by the April 2001 annual report, Washington Mutual was a barn burner. The bank had established an impressive presence in the western states and business was booming. Washington Mutual was among Value Trust's top performers, up 106.2 percent. The stock continued to hold up well in 2001, with a 52-week low of $22.58 and a high of $42.99.

WASTE MANAGEMENT INC.

Another one of Miller's bad-news picks, Waste Management, gave him a lot of headaches before it made a blazing turnaround.

When pressed for information in 1999 about stocks he liked best, Miller dropped the technical explanations and got right to the point: "The stuff I really like is the really bad stuff."[12] By this he meant companies that were absolutely mangled by the market and tragically out of favor. "I really like Waste Management. In the mid-1980s it was the quintessential growth stock. Now it trades at around 16 bucks, or 11 times next year's earnings."

And yet in this case, Miller fell prey to a situation that most investors find difficult to avoid—that of buying too soon. "It's a name that we got involved in way too early. We bought in the $50s initially on the strength of a low multiple and accelerating free cash flow."[13]

Waste Management was clearly a mistake in the low $50s. That enticing cash flow was fantasy. It never materialized. Not long after Miller acquired his chunk of the stock, it was learned—and made public—that the company's accounting was an absolute mess. Additionally, the company experienced integration problems related to its merger with USA Waste Company, system problems, and all manner of management difficulties. (In 1998, USA Waste acquired Waste Management Inc. and adopted its name.) The company announced it would fall short of third-quarter earnings estimates and lowered its numbers for the remainder of 1999 plus the next year. The stock price collapsed as outraged investors dashed for the exit. Some investors were so angry that they filed a class action suit accusing certain managers of anticipating the share price drop and profiting both by insider trading and by collecting stock options and severance pay they didn't deserve. Shareholders eventually won that suit to the tune of $24.6 million, most of which came out of managers' pockets, not company coffers.

Throughout this corporate mayhem, Miller continued to believe in the long-term fundamental economics of the industry and of Waste Management itself.

Regarding the company's fundamentals, landfills are its most valuable asset. Waste Management holds 28 percent of market share in an absolutely essential industry that has no foreign competition. The industry has no dollar risk and no technology risk.

As for industry economics, supply remains limited while demand continues to increase. Waste disposal is an oligopoly industry—not quite the monopoly or "toll booth" that Buffett looks for, but close enough to be an attractive industry. There are only two major players, Waste Management and Allied Waste, a company created by the merger of Browning Ferris and Allied.

Miller's fellow money manager, Mason Hawkins, was attracted to Waste Management, and for similar reasons. Although the price fell drastically, he said, "we think that decline is not indicative of the intrinsic value of the business."[14] Hawkins pointed out that Waste Management was the dominant operator in almost all its regional markets. The company has the best landfill and waste collection assets in the industry—assets that would be nearly impossible to replicate today.

Hawkins regarded the accounting problems as fixable, and, like Miller, he anticipated strong net cash earnings and excellent free cash flow. Before the surprise announcement of accounting deficiencies, Hawkins had about 5 percent of Longleaf Partner's portfolio in WMI. Hawkins felt that the company still had enormous promise and increased his holdings to 14.6 percent while the price was depressed.

Miller agreed that even as the share price dropped, the market was overdiscounting Waste Management, and he kept buying. By 2001, it was Value Trust's largest holding, with more than 6 percent of the fund's assets in this single issue. Miller stayed with the stock during its debacle because he felt that using earnings as a proxy for free cash flow, the company would turn profitable in 2000. And if the company used its $1 billion of free cash flow wisely, it would be a terrific holding.

"If Waste Management takes just 40 percent of its free cash flow and buys small waste companies for cash, that will add about four or five cents after-tax to annual earnings. What you end up with is a business worth in the mid-to-high 20s trading in the mid-teens," said Miller.[15]

Furthermore, because the waste management business has substantial pricing flexibility, Waste Management would be able to implement selective price increases. Miller believed that Waste Management is capable of 20 percent profit margins. Between 2000 and 2001 he bought many millions of additional shares in the low teens.

It seemed like a bright glimmer of hope when Maurice Myers, former chairman of Yellow Corp. (the parent of trucking company Yellow Freight) in November, 1999 was named as Waste Management's new chief executive officer. Miller had confidence in Myers. He was the sixth CEO since May 1996. At least one of the men, John Drury, departed for reasons not directly related to the company's woes. He was forced to leave the job when he was tragically afflicted with brain cancer.

ERROR ANALYSIS

When Miller and his team make an investment mistake, it's usually because the numbers they feed into their models are erroneous.

Waste Management is a disturbing example of how this can happen. When he bought into the company in early 1999 when the stock was trading in the $50s, Miller said, "we believed the shares were worth $60 to $70 based on all the inputs we had from our model. As it turned out, the inputs were totally wrong. Management gave incorrect numbers, so the baseline off which we calculated growth rates and discounted it back to calculate free cash flows was wrong, as were their cash-flow numbers. Even [Waste Management's] historical reported numbers were wrong."[16]

Based on the corrected numbers and the new economic reality the new figures presented, the stock took a nosedive from $50 to the low $20s. "This gives you an idea of how sensitive these numbers are to input changes when you do forward-looking valuation work, like we do," said Miller.[17]

In time, the company made corrections and the stock did well for him. By the March 2001 annual report, Waste Management was among the top performers, with a return of 80.5 percent. In 2001, the company had traded at a 52-week low of $17.13 and a 52-week high of $35.85. By the end of 2001 it was trading at just over $30 with Miller's average cost per share at $18. Miller believes the stock has the potential for a long, high climb. He expects the company's $1 billion cash flow for 2001 to generate both earnings and cash flow growth of 10, 12, or even 15 percent a year over the coming decade. If Miller is correct in this analysis, the share price should track those performance figures as they ascend.

Despite the traumatic experience in the stock, Legg Mason analyst Mark Niemann says the stock was not a high risk, especially when it traded below $20. "The market overreacted to the accounts of scandal," he said. "It's amazing to me more investors didn't load up on it."[18]

EASTMAN KODAK

Miller admits that Eastman Kodak has underperformed the market as far back as most people can remember, but, if you try to think of a company that dominates its industry, Kodak is it. For the most part, investors are worried that digital camera sales will cut into Kodak's traditional camera and film business—a fear that probably is unfounded. Kodak is a leader in digital technology as well as disposable cameras, industrial film, and many other aspects of photography.

Based on his studies of the economics of new technologies, Miller believes that the conventional film business and the digital photography businesses will continue to coexist, since people tend to use each differently. Even with the advent of digital photography, the market for conventional film is huge and global.

"The price of the stock is so low," Miller noted. "They dominate almost the total film market. They have sound underpinnings, and the sales numbers for film and conventional cameras are up. Kodak is worth twice the current price."[19] At the time Miller started talking about it in late 2000, Kodak was selling at around $56 per share, trading at less than 10 times trailing earnings. It traded at that same level in 1995, then peaked at the end of 1996 at around $95 per share. The extremely low share price provided Kodak shares a substantial margin of safety. In 2001, Kodak traded at a high of $63.56, but following the terrorist attacks on September 11, it hit a low of $32.58. Even so, Kodak's share price at the end of that year was down roughly 50 percent from when Miller started buying, and the fund's position was in the red about 40 percent.

Yet Miller continued to buy. Factors leading to Miller's positive take on Kodak are that the company has 20 percent operating margins, 10 percent net margins, earns 30 percent on equity, 20 percent on invested capital, and has generated $1 billion of free cash flow. It was a classic value buy. And, insists Miller, Eastman Kodak wouldn't be going out of business. "Kodak reminds me a lot of IBM in 1993–94 when Louis Gerstner came in. You have a dominant company whose most profitable business is under attack from new technology. Then it was IBM's mainframe business, here it's Kodak's conventional film business. They are a major player, though, in the new technologies, No. 2 or 3 behind Sony or Olympus in the digital-camera area, which we happen to believe is a great and growing area. Nobody is making any money in it, including Sony. As that industry shakes out, ultimately you will make money in it. If it becomes a service-centric business, as it looks like it may, then the potential for margins and additional free cash flow generation at Kodak goes up very significantly."[20]

Miller expects Eastman Kodak to generate about 60 percent of its total current enterprise value in free cash flow between 2001 and 2006. He believes Kodak has a sensible, honest, experienced management team that will allocate capital intelligently. Again, his optimism may be premature. By October 2001, sales had dropped 7 percent from the previous year and layoffs were planned.

TOYS "R" US

In the year 2000, Miller began investing in one of America's favorite retailers, Toys "R" Us. The share price was suffering from competition on the Internet and from the deep discount retailers. Peter Lynch described the company as a classic value buy. "Toys "R" Us was a terrific growth stock in the '80s until Wal-Mart and K-mart started carrying great toys. The stock peaked at $40 in 1992, then went to $9. In the last year [2001] the Nasdaq is down 60 percent, while Toys "R" Us is up from $15 to $25. You just had to keep staying in touch until you saw that the success of their Babies "R" Us stores has been huge."[21]

Toys "R" Us followed the traditional pattern of many of Miller's acquisitions. It was a dud in the beginning, down 37.4 percent for the year ended March 31, 1999. But by March 31, 2001, it bounced up to be with the strongest performers. That year it posted a gain of 69.6 percent. By the fall of 2001, the shares had a 52-week low of $14.50 and a 52-week high of $31 and were trading at around $18.

ALBERTSON'S

Among Bill Miller's old-economy favorites for 2000 and 2001 is the grocery chain Albertson's, a company that once towered as the gold standard of the grocery industry. When in August 1999, the company reported decreased sales and earnings, investors got an excellent opportunity to load up on Albertson's. The stock gradually dropped to around $23 from a 52-week high of $52.25.

The company's shares fell through the floor following a difficult merger in 1999 with American Stores company, operator of among other retailers, Jewel, Lucky, and Osco. Miller felt certain, however, that the company would rebound. "It has a 24-year history of positive shareholder return. We think it has the ability to trade at 10 times what we think it will earn. It will grow 12 to 14 percent over the next few years. It has a low multiple, and a slow, steady pattern."

Though it represented less than 5 percent of Value Trust's assets, in the summer of 2001, Albertson's was among Miller's top 10 holdings. In midsummer, the Boise, Idaho–based company announced a restructuring that would close 165 stores and cut 15 to 20 percent of nonstore jobs. That year, the share price had advanced to $36.99, up from a 52-week low of around $20.

GO YOUR OWN WAY

By January 2001, there was widespread fear that the United States was headed into a recession. That year, when most of the stock market news sounded gloomy, a strange anomaly existed. In late August, the Nasdaq was down 52 percent from its March 10 high. That index definitely was suffering a bear market. The Standard & Poor's 500 index peaked on March 24 at 1,527. It closed down 14.7 percent, which was not good news, but by common definition a market needs to decline by 20 percent before it is considered a bear market. The Dow, unlike the broader averages, was down only 4.5 percent. This did not constitute a cheerful market outlook by any means, but it showed that the market was alive. Because of the dissonance between performances of various indexes, many money managers were fleeing to the safety of the more traditional companies listed on the New York Stock Exchange and represented in the Dow. This was encouraging for value investors, especially those who were unwilling to venture into technology stocks.

As the year 2001 dawned, Louis Rukeyser asked Miller what his single best piece of advice was for the next 12 months. This was his reply:

> "*I*gnore the headlines and be optimistic—because the American economy is the strongest and most innovative in the world, and to take advantage of its wonderful opportunities, investors really need to think long-term and be patient.["](22)

Miller followed his own counsel. Nasdaq stocks were so beaten down in 2000–2001—a loss of more than 50 percent—that the exchange's high-tech-oriented list began to look attractive again. The battered companies list read like a Who's Who of the technology world: Cisco Systems, JDS Uniphase, Motorola, Nortel Networks, and Miller's old friend, MCIWorldCom. It was no wonder that Miller began rebuilding tech and telecom stocks into Value Trust's portfolio. Among his favorites this time were Tellabs and Level 3.

CONCLUSION

It ain't over till it's over.

Yogi Berra

From 1926 through 1999, there were 20 down years for the market, therefore it behooves all investors to expect that the return on their funds will be better in some years than in others. At certain times, the economy, along with investment results, will be downright discouraging.

Bill Miller started his career as a money manager in 1980—the year Ronald Reagan was elected president of the United States. Miller managed money during the recession that was in place when Reagan took office, as well as during the long period of prosperity and the bull market that started in 1982. He continued to manage money through the antitrust breakup of AT&T in 1984; the Black Monday stock market crash of October 19, 1987; the savings and loan crisis that broke in 1988; the 1990 Gulf War; the 1997–1998 Asian financial panic; the collapse of inflated technology stocks; and right through the September 11, 2001 terrorist attacks on the World Trade Center and the Pentagon. That tragedy caused the market to fall more than 14 percent in one week, a decline eclipsed only by a one-week loss of 16 percent during the Great Depression.

Despite the woes of the world and the financial challenges they present, money managers must keep moving forward, and Miller has. Though most of those years his primary fund responsibility, Legg

Mason Value Trust, did very well, Miller did not make money for his mutual fund investors in every year. However, he did minimize losses in years in which stock market investments did poorly. In 1991, he began beating his benchmark index, the S&P 500, and that streak continues today. Miller, who works from an office with a spectacular view of the Baltimore Orioles' Camden Yard stadium, is on his way to becoming the Cal Ripken of the investment world.

IT DEPENDS ON WHEN YOU ASK

The most difficult value principle for the public to accept is that of patience. In a generation of people who are accustomed to instant gratification and for a news media that magnifies quarterly returns, the idea that certain market conditions require a posture of waiting or preparation for the next phase is not easy to sell. Some investors complain that Miller's performance isn't as good as it seems, because positive return depends on getting into the fund at the right time and staying there. Even over the long term, Miller explains that returns are what physicists call "sensitive dependent on initial conditions. It matters to the measurement where the measurement begins. Returns measured from lows to highs give one perspective, those measured on a calendar basis another."[1]

THE STRIKEOUTS

Despite Miller's consistently good record, there are money managers with higher long-term performances. Their long-term numbers are better because their performance is higher than Miller's in some years and lower than the S&P 500 in others. Miller's results are more even and predictable, but he admits to making mistakes with some of his stock picks. He rode his Leslie Fay stock all the way into bankruptcy, and Miller had such confidence in a company called Salant that he followed it into bankruptcy three times before he bailed out.

RISING TO THE NEXT LEVEL

Other critics continue to insist that Miller isn't a value investor at all. At a time when those who studied at the feet of the father of value investing, Benjamin Graham, were sporting gray beards, a relatively young Bill Miller was adapting their philosophy to the realities of a new economy. He studied with contemporary economic thinkers such as Brian Arthur, Hal Varian, and Carl Shapiro, as well as scientists from the disciplines of physics, biology, and other natural sciences. Miller has reconsidered certain old investment ideas. More important, he has embraced new ones, such as the notion that most early leaders in the technology sector were likely to continue as big players. This was contrary to the conventional wisdom that claimed the precocious entries were pioneers, but they made so many mistakes that they soon fell by the wayside, their corpses paving the way for later contenders.[2] Microsoft Corp. and Intel have already disproved the "early entries are losers" theory, while AOL Time Warner and Amazon.com are on the way to confirming it.

Most of all, Miller has decided that technology is too important a driver of economic growth and of value creation to be ignored. A money manager must find some intelligent way to deal with the mysteries and machinations of tech markets.

To be an independent thinker in the investment world requires certain strength of will, a quality that is rarely found. "Warren Buffett captured the essence of the matter when he remarked that in investing it is usually better to fail conventionally than to succeed unconventionally," says Miller. "Or as one fund manager put it recently when asked why he wasn't thinking of investing in Mexico, since undoubtedly there were bargains to be had with many stocks down 70 percent in the past six months [in 1995], 'nobody ever got fired for not investing in Mexico.' "[3]

WANT GROWTH? CONCENTRATE ON VALUE

Miller is undisturbed by the claim that he buys growth, not value stocks. "I've regarded it as a legitimate question of methods. There is some confusion as to what we do."[4]

On the other hand, Miller has often repeated that "we do not believe that carving the world into 'value' or 'growth' is a sensible or useful way to think about the investment process. Growth is an input into the calculation of value."[5]

Despite claims to the contrary, Miller qualifies as a value manager because he buys stocks when they are deeply undervalued and holds on to them for the long term. He uses the traditional value techniques to determine the intrinsic value of a stock, but adds other highly sophisticated measures of value. Like many other value investors, his dogs often dozed on the porch for far too long, but when they awoke, the mongrel stocks tended to move very quickly.

What would make Miller *not* a value investor? Perhaps the fact that he bought into companies that hadn't yet achieved profitability. Traditionally, value assessments are based on measurable data, not on projects or expectations of future performance.

Investors often make the mistaken assumption that price volatility is an investor's enemy. In the *Intelligent Investor*, which was first published in 1949, Benj. Graham declared that as long as the earning power of an investor's holdings remains satisfactory, he should ignore the vagaries of the stock market. In fact, the wise investor turns price swings to his advantage, buying on the downturn and selling on the upswing. "The investor who permits himself to be stampeded or unduly worried by the unjustified market declines in his holdings is perversely transforming his basic advantage into a basic disadvantage. Price fluctuations have only one significant meaning to the true investor. They provide him with an opportunity to buy wisely when prices fall sharply and to sell wisely when they advance a great deal."[6]

Miller doesn't try to outguess the stock market. "We have learned over the years that predicting the market is futile; understanding it is challenge enough."[7]

Once Miller has decided to buy a stock, he does not hesitate to let his gains ride. America Online was a major influence on Special Investment Trust's results around the turn of the century. Miller bought a nominal position in the company originally, but the stock grew in dollar value and gradually represented a larger and larger percentage of the portfolio's assets. By the spring of 2000, it represented a whopping 22.5 percent. Holding on was incredibly smart in 1999, when the AOL position was up 750 percent. Investors got a little nervous the next year when the stock declined 8.9 percent during the trust's fiscal year. But averaged out over a longer term, AOL was a winner.

REVIEWING THE CRITERIA

When choosing an individual stock, Miller looks for companies selling at large discounts to his assessment of underlying or intrinsic value. In situations where it makes sense, Miller looks at historical patterns of valuation. Rather than relying entirely on data that tell about the company's past performance, Miller strives to use information that reveals something about future company performance. He builds models based on various scenarios, using different end points, growth rates, discount rates, and other variables.

Because the value of any asset is equal to the cash you take out of it over time, one of the most important aspects of Miller's analysis is measuring a stock's value based on the present value of the free cash flow it generates. Free cash flow is simply the discretionary cash that management has available with which to do one or a combination of four things: (1) buy back stock, (2) pay down debt, (3) acquire other businesses, or (4) pay dividends. Cash flow numbers obviously can be manipulated. But the point of the matter is that a business with growing and predictable free cash flow is worth more than a business that generates minimal or no cash. In an attempt to determine the long-term prospects of a business, Miller calculates the price a stock should be selling for (its present value) based on future earnings expectations, discounted by a forecasted growth rate.

This said, Miller admonishes that numbers alone, especially those derived from simplistic calculations, can never tell the whole story. When in the spring of 2000 the *New York Times* proclaimed that the value investing game was over, Miller came back with an ironic reply: "We have no idea what the new game will be. By 'game,' we mean the simple-minded rule that will explain, after the fact, what you should have done to beat the market during the period in question."[8]

While it won't work to reduce Miller's philosophy to mere bullet points, there are some guidelines that we can glean from his words and actions. He buys a company, not the stock, and the selection should be made with business principles in mind. Miller factors the following elements into the selection process.

BILL MILLER'S INVESTMENT PRINCIPLES

- **Evolve the investment strategy as the environment changes, always keeping a value orientation**

  Miller draws inspiration and insights from every field of knowledge. His pragmatic mindset and multidisciplinary thinking process have kept him from being wedded to particular metrics/analytical techniques, or arbitrarily excluding industries, such as technology, from the quest for bargains.

- **Adopt the strengths, but not the weaknesses, of the competition: the S&P 500**

  Like the S&P 500, Miller invests for the long-term remaining fully invested with low turnover. He lets the winners run, while selectively paring the losers. But he uses a more sophisticated business selection strategy and is highly sensitive to valuation, buying undervalued businesses and selling significantly overvalued ones.

- **Observe, but don't forecast, the economy and the stock market**

  The complex interaction of so many people and organizations, all adapting to better compete with one another, results in large-scale unpredictable behavior, including booms and crashes (such as the dot.com bubble and the 1987 one-day stock market crash). Cause and effect are not simplistically linked, so forecasting is folly. Yet observing these complex adaptive systems, cognizant of how complex behavior emerges and feedback loops amplify or dampen effects, still yields insights for Miller.

- **Seek companies with superior business models and high returns on capital over time**

   Miller looks for businesses with sustainable competitive advantages; strong, shareholder-oriented management; and a market position that enables them to play offense, not defense. He focuses on the long-term underlying economics of the business rather than the short-term accounting.

- **Take advantage of, rather than fall victim to, psychologically driven thinking errors**

   Common thinking errors that Miller looks for include overconfidence, overreaction, loss aversion, mental accounting, magical thinking, false patterns, and crowd psychology.

- **Buy businesses at a large discount to the central tendency of their intrinsic value**

   Miller values each business using multiple methods (multiples, discounted cash flow, private market value, etc.) and multiple scenarios. He compares the distribution of estimated intrinsic values with what the market is discounting. If the market's expectations for a company's future cash flows (implied by its low stock price) are significantly below the cluster of intrinsic values supported by carefully evaluated evidence, then he considers buying.

- **Win with the lowest average cost**

   Confident in his exhaustive analysis, Miller continues buying as a matter of principle and profit as a stock price drops. "Munching" enables him to earn a market-beating return even on stocks bought too soon, such as Waste Management, which actually dropped as much as 75 percent after he began buying it. Yet, the Value Trust's return on its average Waste Management price was 18 percent in mid-November 2001, while the S&P 500 had dropped 9 percent over the same period.

- **Cultivate a focused portfolio of 15 to 50 businesses**

   Miller concentrates the portfolio on his best ideas, investing higher percentages in the best of the best. Most professional investors diversify too much—buying so many stocks (typically hundreds) that they lack the time to truly understand them. Their portfolios avoid the higher volatility of a focused portfolio over the short-term, but typically have returns below the market average after expenses.

- **Maximize the expected return on the portfolio, *not* the frequency of correct picks**

  Most people try to maximize the number of times they are right because the psychological pain of a loss is twice the pleasure from a similar gain. Yet the frequency of success is much less important than people believe. The key is how much you make when you are right. Like Buffett, Miller puts big bets on high probability events. But he also makes a collection of bets on companies where the probability of his being right on any individual bet, even with all his research, is low. But the potential payoff from any of these bets is enormous—as much as 2 to 40 times the original investment.

- **Sell when 1) the company reaches fair value (but valuation changes over time); 2) you find a better bargain; 3) the fundamental logic for the investment changes**

  Most people sell too early to earn 20 plus times their investment, unlike Miller who earned those returns on AOL, Dell, MBNA, Danaher, and others. Traditional value investors, for example, sold Dell when the P/E multiple reached 12, its traditional high, missing its superior business model and rapidly rising return on capital, which fueled a dramatic rise in its stock price. Other investors buy and hold, but forget to sell to capture return. Miller, however, sold most of his Dell and AOL as technology peaked in early 2000.

THE BOY SCOUT PRINCIPLES

Bill Miller's investment approach isn't for everyone. It entails hard work, attention, diligence, patience, and supreme self-confidence.

But his methods also have their rewards. They are ideal for those who enjoy research, analysis, delving into the underlying reality of a business, and who welcome constant self-education and reeducation. You learned it yesterday? Relearn it tomorrow.

In the past decade, and certainly after the dawn of the new millennium, the investment world has changed. John Seely Brown of Xerox PARC spoke the following words in the late 1990s, but by 2001, his words had even deeper meaning: "In the old economy, the challenge for management is to make product. Now the challenge for management is to make sense."[9]

THE INFORMATION AGE

It has not required great imagination to understand that as the world goes through a cultural and economic shift, from analog to digital, from snail mail to e-mail, from libraries to the Internet, almost all aspects of life are changing. One of the most remarkable occurences is the rapidity with which information is transmitted worldwide, not to mention the overwhelming amount of information that is now available. Most of us can't keep up with our reading or information gathering. The investment world is not left out of this transfiguration. It has been enormously impacted by scientific advances, which permit trading and even day trading from home, allow portfolio tracking within minutes of real time, and provide almost instantaneous access to Securities and Exchange Commission reports along with many other innovations.

It seems only logical that a more complicated investment world will require a swifter and smarter approach to investment decisions. That's one reason Bill Miller's multifactor security analysis is appealing. It is a complex, intellectual method for complex times in which there is intense focus on intellectual growth, intellectual accomplishments, and intellectual property. It's what comes out of our brains that matters in today's world. Any time that decisions must be made, information is critical, and when the information load turns to overload, clever management of information is essential. The danger in following Miller's style is that some investors will get caught up and become fully engaged in the analytic process and lose sight of the goal. As more information flows in, decision making will be increasingly difficult, especially for those investors suffering from analysis paralysis. The Miller method makes enormous sense as long as information assessment doesn't become a substitute for thinking and action.

9/11—THE DAY THE WORLD CHANGED

Investors already were having a difficult time coming to terms with the correction in high tech markets of the end of the century. Then came the disastrous events of September 11, 2001, and the impact that terrorism had on the financial markets. Miller believed that equity markets bottomed in the spring of 2001 (markets tend to bottom about six months before the economy reaches the lowest point in its cycle), but the bottom was tested again in late September.

The third quarter of 2001 will be forever identified with what happened that day, he observed. "September 11 had the effect of shocking consumers from a psychological standpoint and changing the valuations of certain industries—travel, hotel, defense, security," said Miller. "These changes in valuations occurred quickly and the prices of those companies quickly reflected the event."[10]

While many investors sought safety in more liquid, shorter-term and higher quality assets, the attack on the very heart of Wall Street catalyzed a bottom in the market and represented the low for the bear cycle that began in March, 2000.

And yet, said Miller, just as people were unduly optimistic in the fall of 2000, they were unduly pessimistic in the fall of 2001. A series of interest rate cuts, government economic incentive packages and corporate retrenchment were among the signs of a pending recovery. For a value investor like Miller, the key question loomed larger than ever: What companies are selling at deeply discounted prices and what are the prospects for future profitability? Although Miller didn't expect a quick return to the glory days of the late 1990s, he began predicting that technology, telecommunications, and financial services stocks, along with junk bonds, would take wing in 2002. He started to load up his Legg Mason funds with additional shares of Nextel, Waste Management Inc., Citigroup, and Eastman Kodak. He took positions in stocks like Corning and Comverse.

Miller was acting on his own advice that appeared at the end of Chapter 7. "Ignore the headlines and be optimistic, because the American economy is the strongest and most innovative in the world, and to take advantage of its wonderful opportunities investors really need to think long term and be patient."[11]

After all, to quote Yogi Berra, "Even if this world was perfect, it wouldn't be." Miller continues to keep an alert and open mind when considering potential changes that could confront all investors in the twenty-first century. But he also deferred on this point to another of his favorite philosophers: "As William James would say, we can't really draw any final conclusions about anything."[12]

APPENDIX 1: LEGG MASON VALUE TRUST FUND HOLDINGS

PORTFOLIO OF INVESTMENTS—1982

American Cyanamid
American Telephone & Telegraph
Ball Corporation
Continental Group
CSX Corporation
First Maryland Bancorp
W.R. Grace & Company
Household International Corp.
JWT Group, Inc.
Maryland National Corporation
Norfolk Southern Corporation
PPG Industries, Inc.
SCM Corporation
Sherwin-Williams Company
Union Carbide Corporation
Westinghouse Electric Corp.

PORTFOLIO OF INVESTMENTS—1996

AMBAC, Inc.
Amgen, Inc.
Bank of America Corporation
Bank of Boston Corporation
The Bear Stearns Companies, Inc.
The Chase Manhattan Corporation

Chemical Banking Corporation
Chrysler Corporation (later became DaimlerChrysler)
Circus Circus Enterprises, Inc. (later became Mandalay Group Inc.)
Citicorp (later became Citigroup)
Coltec Industries, Inc.
Columbia/HCA Healthcare Corporation
Danaher Corporation
Dell Computer Corporation
Digital Equipment Corporation
DuPont (E.I.) De Nemours
Federal Home Loan Mortgage Corporation
Federal National Mortgage Association (Fannie Mae)
Fleet Financial Group, Inc.
General Motors Corporation
Humana, Inc.
International Business Machines Corporation
The Kroger Company
Lloyds TSB Group plc
MBIA, Inc.
MBNA Corporation
MCI Communications Corporation
Nike, Inc.
Nokia Corporation
Pepsico
Philip Morris Companies, Inc.
Philips Electronics N.V.
Provident Bankshares Corporation
Reebok International Ltd
RJR Nabisco Holdings Corporation (now called R.J. Reynolds Tobacco Holdings Inc.)
Standard Federal Bancorporation
Teléfonos de Mexico S.A.
The Walt Disney Company
Warner-Lambert Company
Zions Bancorporation

PORTFOLIO OF INVESTMENTS—1999

AMBAC Financial Group, Inc.
America Online, Inc.
Amgen, Inc.
Bank of America Corporation
BankBoston Corporation

Bank One Corporation
The Bear Stearns Companies, Inc.
Berkshire Hathaway Inc.
The Chase Manhattan Corporation
Circus Circus Enterprises, Inc. (later Mandalay Group Inc.)
Citigroup, Inc.
Compaq Computer Corporation
Conseco, Inc.
Danaher Corporation
Dell Corporation
Fannie Mae
First Data Corporation
Fleet Financial Corporation
Foundation Health Systems, Inc.
Freddie Mac
Gateway 2000, Inc.
General Motors Corporation
Hilton Hotels Corporation
International Business Machines Corporation
Koninklijke (Royal) Philips Electronics N.V.
Kroger Company
The Learning Company, Inc.
Lloyds TSB Group plc
MBIA, Inc.
Metro-Goldwyn Mayer, Inc.
MGIC Investment Corporation
MBNA Corporation
MGM Grand, Inc.
Mirage Resorts, Incorporated
Pepsico, Inc.
Philip Morris Companies
Starwood Hotels & Resorts Worldwide, Inc.
Storage Technology Corporation
Toys "R" Us, Inc.
United Health Care Corporation
Washington Mutual, Inc.
Western Digital Corporation
WPP Group plc.
Zions Bancorporation

PORTFOLIO OF INVESTMENTS—2001

Albertson's, Inc.
Amazon.com, Inc.

AOL Time Warner, Inc.
Bank of America Corporation
Bank One Corporation
The Bear Stearns Companies, Inc.
Berkshire Hathaway, Inc.
Citigroup, Inc.
Corning, Inc.
Danaher Corporation
Dell Computer Corporation
Eastman Kodak Company
Fannie Mae
Fleet Boston Financial Corporation
Gateway, Inc.
General Motors Corporation
Healthnet Inc.
International Business Machines Corp.
J.P. Morgan Chase & Company
The Kroger Company
Level 3 Communications, Inc.
Lloyds TLC Group plc.
MBNA Corporation
McKesson HBOC, Inc.
Metro-Goldwyn-Mayer, Inc.
MGIC Investment Corporation
MGM Mirage, Inc.
Nextel Communications, Inc.
Starwood Hotels and Resorts Worldwide, Inc.
Storage Technology Corporation
Teléfonos de Mexico S A
Tellabs, Inc.
Toys "R" Us, Inc.
United Health Group, Inc.
Washington Mutual, Inc.
Waste Management, Inc.
WPP Group plc

APPENDIX 2:
BILL MILLER AND
LEGG MASON MUTUAL
FUNDS CHRONOLOGY

1899—George Mackubin & Co. (a predecessor to Legg & Co.), a Maryland broker-dealer, was founded in Baltimore.

1972—Miller graduated from Washington and Lee University with degrees in European history and economics.

1981—Miller joined Legg Mason as an understudy to research chief Ernie Kiehne.

1982—On April 16, Miller helped Ernie Kiehne launch the Legg Mason Value Trust as a way to showcase the company's research capabilities.

1985—To resolve conflicts of interest, Miller ceased doing sell-side research and gave his full attention to the Value Trust.

—Miller buys Fannie Mae after Peter Lynch pointed out its superior business model and Miller subsequently researched its economic advantages.

1987—When Miller read an article in the *New York Times* on chaos theory, he learned about the innovative Santa Fe Institute.

1990—In October, Bill Miller became the sole manager of Legg Mason Value Trust.

1992—Miller made his first visit to the Santa Fe Institute by invitation from then Citibank chairman John Reed.

1996—Miller took his first flyer in America Online.

—As Las Vegas hotels madly expanded and gaming company stocks were shunned because of the debt load, Miller began buying Circus Circus, Mirage Resorts, and MGM Grand shares.

1998—Morningstar named Miller its Domestic Equity Fund Manager of the Year.

1999—Miller bought shares of Waste Management Inc. in the $50 range, and shortly afterward the stock went into a severe tailspin on the news that accounting numbers were wrong and earnings projections were far too high.

—Miller surprised the investment world by taking a major position in Amazon.com.

—Washington Mutual and other financial services companies were purchased for the Value Trust portfolio.

—Mutual fund managers voted Bill Miller as Morningstar's Portfolio Manager of the Decade.

—Legg Mason launched Miller's newest fund, Opportunity Trust.

2000—In January and February, Miller began backing away from high-tech stocks because of excessively high valuations, turning his attention to old technology stocks.

—When Miller outperformed the S&P 500 index for the ninth consecutive year, he replaced Peter Lynch as the record holder for that achievement.

—Nancy Dennin was named assistant portfolio manager of Value Trust.

—Masters' Select Equity named Bill Miller as its latest fund manager, replacing Robert Sanborn.

2001—Lisa Rapuano took full charge of the fund that she had helped Miller manage, the Legg Mason Special Investment Trust.

—By January 2001, there were widespread fears of recessions. The Federal Reserve began dropping interest rates, but the stock markets continued to decline.

—September 11, 2001, terrorists flew hijacked airliners into the twin towers of the World Trade Center and into the Pentagon. A fourth airliner, supposedly headed for the White House, crashed in a field in Pennsylvania. U.S. stock markets were closed until September 17, and after opening, suffered a 14 percent decline in the first week of trading.

APPENDIX 3:
WEB ADDRESSES

www.capatcolumbia.com—site for Columbia University Professor Michael
    Mauboussin

www.cbs.marketwatch.com—extensive mutual fund data

www.dividenddiscountmodel.com—information about the dividend dis-
    count model

www.leggmasonfunds.com—Legg Mason's own company web site

www.nasdaq.com

www.santafe.edu—the Santa Fe Institute site

www.stern.nyu.edu/-adamodar/—a somewhat simplified discounted cash
    flow model useful for evaluating the value of a stock

www.ValuePro.net—offers basic software for figuring discounted cash flows
    that may not be sophisticated enough for final analysis but will help a
    beginner learn

APPENDIX 4: CHARTS

Figure 1   Albertson's, Inc. (NYSE—ABS)

Market Cap: $14,819,410,000

Revenue (Fiscal 2001): $36,762,000,000

Albertson's operates about 2,500 supermarkets in 36 states under names such as Albertson's, Acme, and Jewel. More than half of these locations are combination food and drugstores, and about 800 are stand-alone drugstores operating under the Osco and Sav-On flags. In February 2001, Albertson's had 235,000 employees.

Stock History

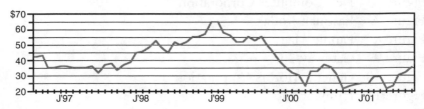

Key Ratios and Statistics

Valuation (ratios)

Price/Earnings	Price/Sales	Price/Book	Price/Cash Flow
19.58	0.41	2.55	8.44

Per Share ($)

Earnings	Sales	Book	Cash Flow	Cash	Return/ Equity	Return/ Assets	Return/ Investment
1.87	89.57	14.35	4.33	1.12	13.42	4.87	6.29

Profitability (%, 12 months to August 2001)

Gross Margin	Operating Margin	Profit Margin
28.50	4.64	2.08

Growth Rates (%)

Sales	1 year −1.91	3 years 2.81	5 years 23.91
EPS	1 year 81.19	3 years 0.97	5 years 0.00

Miller's assessment of Albertson's:

It has a 24-year history of positive shareholder return. He believes it has the potential to trade at 10 times expected earnings and will grow 12 to 14 percent in the early 2000s. It has a low multiple with a slow but steady growth pattern.

Figure 2   Amazon.com, Inc. (NASDAQ—AMZN)

Market Cap: $4,443,610,000

Revenue (2001 through July): $1,367,981,000

Amazon.com, Inc., is an online retailer offering items including books, music, DVDs/videos, toys, electronics, software, and home products, prescription drugs, and film processing. Amazon owns stakes in on-line sellers of prescription drugs, wine, wedding services, and more. Amazon had 9,000 employees at the end of year 2000.

Stock History

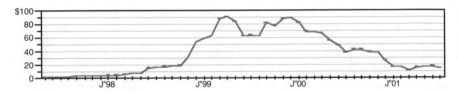

Key Ratios and Statistics

Valuation (ratios)

Price/Earnings	Price/Sales	Price/Book	Price/Cash Flow
N/A	1.47	N/A	N/A

Per Share ($)

Earnings	Sales	Book	Cash Flow	Cash	Return/ Equity	Return/ Assets	Return/ Investment
−3.31	8.35	−3.95	−2.31	1.68	N/A	−54.23	−84.93

Profitability (%, 12 months to August 2001)

Gross Margin	Operating Margin	Profit Margin
25.31	−28.27	−35.20

Growth Rates (%)

Sales	1 year 68.43	3 years 165.38	5 years 457.91
EPS	N/A	N/A	N/A

Miller's assessment of Amazon.com:

Though Amazon was not yet profitable, when Miller purchased it in 1999, he saw a company with a head start that would give it a franchise with a critical retail function. It also had established profitability in key market segments.

Figure 3   AOL/Time Warner (NYSE—AOL)

Market Cap: $200,611,190,000

Revenue (2001 through July): $18,282,000,000

AOL/Time Warner is the parent company of America Online, Inc. and Time Warner Inc. The company is engaged in AOL Internet services, cable, filmed entertainment, television networks, music, and publishing. AOL operates an on-line e-mail service, owns Compuserve, and brings several other interactive on-line services to the AOL Time Warner fold. At the end of year 2000, AOL/Time Warner had 88,500 employees.

Stock History

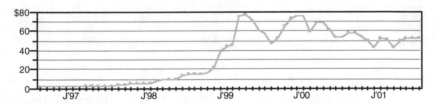

Appendix 4   Charts

Key Ratios and Statistics

Valuation (ratios)

Price/Earnings	Price/Sales	Price/Book	Price/Cash Flow
N/A	6.10	1.29	54.92

Per Share ($)

Earnings	Sales	Book	Cash Flow	Cash	Return/ Equity	Return/ Assets	Return/ Investment
−0.03	7.41	35.12	0.82	0.31	−1.43	−0.85	−0.91

Profitability (%, 12 months to August 2001)

Gross Margin	Operating Margin	Profit Margin
41.21	7.49	−2.97

Growth Rates (%)

Sales	1 year 11.87	3 years 35.24	5 years 47.75
EPS	1 year −6.30	3 years N/A	5 years 92.21

Miller's assessment of AOL/Time Warner:

Miller made AOL a core holding in 1996 because it had captured 40 percent of the market, a position that would be difficult for competitors to usurp.

Figure 4   Bank One (NYSE—ONE)

Market Cap: $42,461,030,000

Revenue (2001 through July): $9,306,000,000

Bank One, the number 5 bank in the United States, is a multibank holding company with some 1,800 branches in 14 mostly midwestern and southeastern states, and provides domestic retail banking, finance and credit card; worldwide corporate and institutional banking; and trust/investment management services. Bank One had 80,778 employees at the end of 2000.

Stock History

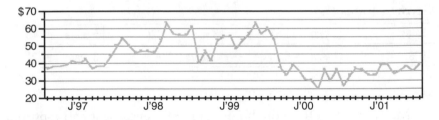

Key Ratios and Statistics

Valuation (ratios)

Price/Earnings	Price/Sales	Price/Book	Price/Cash Flow
29.66	2.16	2.21	20.71

Per Share ($)

Earnings	Sales	Book	Cash Flow	Cash	Return/ Equity	Return/ Assets	Return/ Investment
1.23	16.83	16.49	1.76	15.80	7.66	0.53	2.51

Profitability (%, 12 months to August 2001)

Gross Margin	Operating Margin	Profit Margin
N/A	28.04	7.40

Growth Rates (%)

Sales	1 year	16.10	3 years	4.60	5 years	21.48
EPS	1 year	N/A	3 years	N/A	5 years	N/A

Miller's assessment of Bank One:

When he bought his shares in July, 2000, it was severely marked down because of disruption in foreign banking markets. He expected interest rates to fall, giving bank earnings a big boost.

Figure 5   Citigroup Inc. (NYSE—C)

Market Cap: $251,679,930,000

Revenue (2001 through July): $17,173,000,000

Citigroup Inc. provides a range of financial services, including banking, insurance, and investment services, to consumers and corporate customers around the world. Subsidiaries include Salomon Smith Barney (brokerage), Associates First Capital (consumer lending), and Travelers Property Casualty (insurance). As of the end of 2000, Citigroup had 233,000 employees.

Stock History

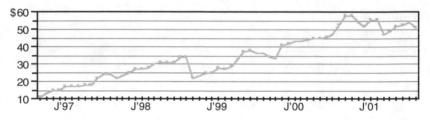

Key Ratios and Statistics

Valuation (ratios)

Price/Earnings	Price/Sales	Price/Book	Price/Cash Flow
18.94	N/A	3.77	14.53

Per Share ($)

Earnings	Sales	Book	Cash Flow	Cash	Return/ Equity	Return/ Assets	Return/ Investment
2.64	N/A	13.29	3.44	2.86	23.69	1.62	9.60

Profitability (%, 12 months to August 2001)

Gross Margin	Operating Margin	Profit Margin
N/A	35.01	N/A

Growth Rates (%)

Sales	1 year	18.10	3 years	15.54	5 years	11.83
EPS	1 year	19.54	3 years	24.03	5 years	19.07

Miller's assessment of Citigroup:

In 1992, Citibank's price was extremely low, but management, which Miller admired, had embraced cost controls he felt would turn this global franchise around. Citigroup was again undervalued in 2001 and Miller bought it after the September 11 terrorist attack.

Figure 6   Dell Computer Corporation (NASDAQ—DELL)

Market Cap: $71,494,750,000

Revenue (2001 through July): $8,028,000,000

Dell designs, develops, manufactures, markets, services, and supports a range of computer systems, including desktop, notebooks, and enterprise systems, including servers and workstations. Dell also markets software, peripherals, and related service and support. As of February 2001, Dell had 40,000 employees.

Stock History

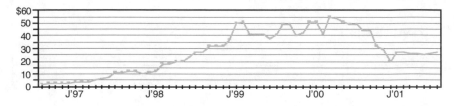

Appendix 4   Charts

Key Ratios and Statistics

Valuation (ratios)

Price/Earnings	Price/Sales	Price/Book	Price/Cash Flow
34.72	2.32	12.98	31.13

Per Share ($)

Earnings	Sales	Book	Cash Flow	Cash	Return/ Equity	Return/ Assets	Return/ Investment
0.79	11.86	2.12	0.88	2.02	37.20	16.64	30.81

Profitability (%, 12 months to August 2001)

Gross Margin	Operating Margin	Profit Margin
19.61	8.05	6.66

Growth Rates (%)

Sales	1 year	26.21	3 years	37.28	5 years	43.20
EPS	1 year	33.22	3 years	36.51	5 years	58.26

Miller's assessment of Dell:

The stock was cheap in 1996 because of worries of a cyclical downturn in personal computer sales. He decided the PC industry was a commodity business and that Dell, a low-cost producer, would be among the few dominant leaders.

Figure 7   Eastman Kodak (NYSE—EK)

Market Cap: $13,602,220,000

Revenue (2001 through July): $6,567,000,000

Eastman Kodak Company develops, manufactures, and markets consumer, professional, health, and other imaging products and services. Kodak is the world's number 1 maker of photographic film and also makes digital and traditional cameras and other products for both amateur and professional photographers. Eastman Kodak had 78,400 employees at the end of year 2000.

Stock History

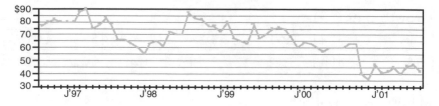

Key Ratios and Statistics

Valuation (ratios)

Price/Earnings	Price/Sales	Price/Book	Price/Cash Flow
17.60	1.01	4.17	8.07

Per Share ($)

Earnings	Sales	Book	Cash Flow	Cash	Return/ Equity	Return/ Assets	Return/ Investment
2.66	46.34	11.21	5.79	1.00	22.27	5.54	9.58

Profitability (%, 12 months to August 2001)

Gross Margin	Operating Margin	Profit Margin
38.89	10.38	5.82

Growth Rates (%)

Sales	1 year −0.67	3 years −1.26	5 years −1.73
EPS	1 year 5.98	3 years 573.82	5 years 4.84

Miller's assessment of Eastman Kodak:

The stock was deeply depressed as the new century began, but the company had solid underpinnings. It dominates almost the total film market and film and camera sales were up. Miller felt Kodak was worth twice the price he paid.

Figure 8   Fannie Mae (NYSE—FNM)

Market Cap: $79,179,000,000

Revenue (2001 through July): $24,965,000,000

Formerly the Federal National Mortgage Association, Fannie Mae is a public company whose existence is mandated by the U.S. government. Fannie Mae provides financial products and services that increase the availability and affordability of housing for low, moderate, and middle-income Americans. Fannie Mae had 4,100 employees at the end of the year 2000.

Stock History

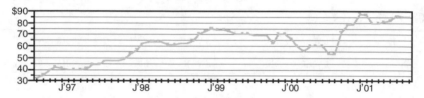

Key Ratios and Statistics

Valuation (ratios)

Price/Earnings	Price/Sales	Price/Book	Price/Cash Flow
16.48	1.65	4.62	4.92

Per Share ($)

Earnings	Sales	Book	Cash Flow	Cash	Return/ Equity	Return/ Assets	Return/ Investment
4.80	47.83	17.11	16.09	59.02	28.70	0.74	1.33

Profitability (%, 12 months to August 2001)

Gross Margin	Operating Margin	Profit Margin
N/A	13.94	10.32

Growth Rates (%)

Sales	1 year	19.26	3 years	16.65	5 years	14.66
EPS	1 year	15.27	3 years	14.83	5 years	17.12

Miller's assessment of Fannie Mae:

This company is a perennial favorite of value investors, and Miller was able to buy it several times at an advantageous price due to the general decline in the financial stock sector. The fund has earned more than 50x its original investment.

Figure 9   Gateway, Inc. (NYSE—GTW)

Market Cap: $3,295,770,000

Revenue (2001 through July): $3,534,385,000

Gateway develops, markets, manufactures, and supports a broad line of desktop and portable PCs and PC-related products used by individuals, businesses, government agencies, and educational institutions. Gateway also markets products through its own Gateway Country stores. Gateway sells third-party peripherals such as CD-ROM drives and offers services such as training, support, and financing.

Stock History

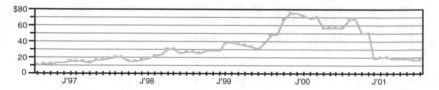

Key Ratios and Statistics

Valuation (ratios)

Price/Earnings	Price/Sales	Price/Book	Price/Cash Flow
N/A	0.39	1.78	N/A

Per Share ($)

Earnings	Sales	Book	Cash Flow	Cash	Return/ Equity	Return/ Assets	Return/ Investment
−1.55	26.19	5.73	−0.87	3.18	−22.58	−12.52	−20.48

Profitability (%, 12 months to July 2001)

Gross Margin	Operating Margin	Profit Margin
17.80	−5.49	−5.82

Growth Rates (%)

Sales	1 year	7.09	3 years	15.12	5 years	21.17
EPS	1 year	−42.00	3 years	29.53	5 years	6.94

Miller's assessment of this company:

Gateway was selling at a low 17 times forecasted earnings in mid-2001. Management had refocused and on the balance sheet it seemed earnings would quickly improve.

Figure 10   General Motors Corporation (NYSE—GM)

Market Cap: $34,506,310,000

Revenue (2000): $42,615,000,000

General Motors Corp. designs, manufactures, and markets automobiles, trucks, and related parts, designs and manufactures locomotives and heavy-duty transmissions, and operates a financial services and insurance company. At the end of year 2000, General Motors had 386,000 employees.

Stock History

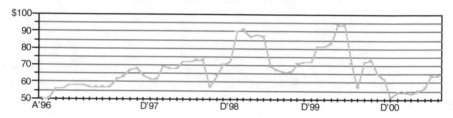

Key Ratios and Statistics

Valuation (ratios)

Price/Earnings	Price/Sales	Price/Book	Price/Cash Flow
34.72	2.32	12.98	31.13

Per Share ($)

Earnings	Sales	Book	Cash Flow	Cash	Return/ Equity	Return/ Assets	Return/ Investment
0.79	11.86	2.12	0.88	2.02	37.20	16.64	30.81

Profitability (%, 12 months to July 2001)

Gross Margin	Operating Margin	Profit Margin
19.61	8.05	6.66

Growth Rates (%)

Sales %	1 year 26.21	2 years 37.28	3 years 43.20
EPS %	1 year 33.2	2 years 36.51	3 years 58.26

Miller's assessment of GM:

Because of accounting changes required by regulators in the early 1990s, GM's book value collapsed from $55 to $5. Miller felt that the change, which impacted GM's share price, did not reflect the underlying reality of the company.

Figure 11   Humana Inc. (NYSE—HUM)

Market Cap: $1,580,630,000

Revenue (2001 through July): $2,445,000,000

Humana Inc. is a health services company that facilitates the delivery of health care services through networks of providers to approximately 5.9 million members, primarily through HMOs and PPOs. Humana also provides dental, group life, and disability insurance. Humana had 15,600 employees at the end of 2001.

Stock History

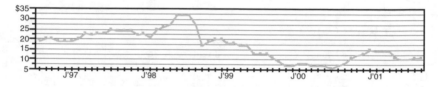

Key Ratios and Statistics

Valuation (ratios)

Price/Earnings	Price/Sales	Price/Book	Price/Cash Flow
16.17	0.15	1.13	15.37

Per Share ($)

Earnings	Sales	Book	Cash Flow	Cash	Return/ Equity	Return/ Assets	Return/ Investment
0.58	61.85	8.26	0.61	11.65	7.18	2.29	6.48

Profitability (%, 12 months to July 2001)

Gross Margin	Operating Margin	Profit Margin
N/A	1.52	0.93

Growth Rates (%)

Sales	1 year 3.97	3 years 9.37	5 years 17.46
EPS	1 year N/A	3 years −19.75	5 years −14.12

Miller's assessment of Humana:

Investors got scared of health care companies in the early 1990s because of health care reforms planned by the Clinton administration, even those with solid financials such as Humana. Miller sold Humana in 1997.

Figure 12   The Kroger Company (NYSE—KR)

Market Cap: $20,613,530,000

Revenue (through July 2001): $15,102,000,000

The Kroger Company is a supermarket grocery retailer and also a manufacturer and processor of food for sale by its supermarkets. The company operates 2,354 supermarkets and has 312,000 employees.

Stock History

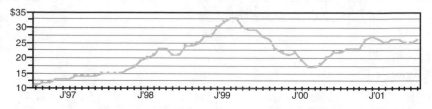

Key Ratios and Statistics

Valuation (ratios)

Price/Earnings	Price/Sales	Price/Book	Price/Cash Flow
19.89	0.43	6.63	10.25

Per Share ($)

Earnings	Sales	Book	Cash Flow	Cash	Return/ Equity	Return/ Assets	Return/ Investment
1.29	59.13	3.87	2.50	0.20	37.67	6.04	8.86

Profitability (%, 12 months to July 2001)

Gross Margin	Operating Margin	Profit Margin
26.99	5.05	2.18

Growth Rates (%)

Sales	1 year	8.04	3 years	4.38	5 years	14.25
EPS	1 year	43.25	3 years	20.66	5 years	8.84

Miller's assessment of Kroger:

Unable to keep pace with tech stocks, old-economy stocks took a beating at the end of the 1990s. When techs began to falter, Kroger was among the high-quality undervalued alternatives. The stock suffered again in 2001 because of severe competition.

199

Figure 13   McKesson Corporation (NYSE—MCK)

Market Cap: $11,406,720,000

Revenue (Fiscal 2001): $42,010,000,000

McKesson is a health care supply management company. The company also provides software solutions, technological innovations, and comprehensive services to the health care industry. Other subsidiaries distribute medical and surgical products to the health care industry. As of March 2001, McKesson had 23,000 employees.

Stock History

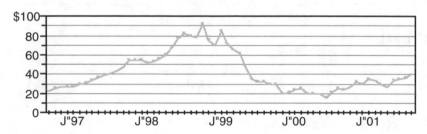

Appendix 4   Charts

Key Ratios and Statistics

Valuation (ratios)

Price/Earnings	Price/Sales	Price/Book	Price/Cash Flow
N/A	0.27	3.15	48.78

Per Share ($)

Earnings	Sales	Book	Cash Flow	Cash	Return/ Equity	Return/ Assets	Return/ Investment
0.03	150.76	12.69	0.82	0.84	-0.03	0.05	0.10

Profitability (%, 12 months to August 2001)

Gross Margin	Operating Margin	Profit Margin
5.74	0.30	0.01

Growth Rates (%)

Sales	1 year 14.51	3 years 23.87	5 years 26.51
EPS	N/A	N/A	N/A

Miller's assessment of McKesson:

Good company, out of favor. Miller bought this stock in 2000 when he made the flight from tech to traditional value.

Figure 14   Mandalay Resort Group (NYSE—MBG)

Market Cap: $1,869,640,000

Revenue (2001 through July): $2,524,224,000

Mandalay Resort Group (formerly Circus Circus Enterprises) is a ho-tel-casino operator that operates 16 properties with more than 27,000 guest rooms and more than one million square feet of casino space in Nevada, Mississippi, Illinois, and Michigan. Mandalay Resort Group had 35,000 employees at the end of 2001.

Stock History

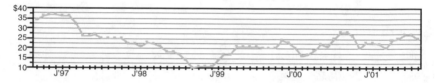

Key Ratios and Statistics

Valuation (ratios)

Price/Earnings	Price/Sales	Price/Book	Price/Cash Flow
16.50	0.76	1.74	5.79

Per Share ($)

Earnings	Sales	Book	Cash Flow	Cash	Return/ Equity	Return/ Assets	Return/ Investment
1.52	32.87		4.33	2.25	11.14	2.76	2.96

Profitability (%, 12 months to July 2001)

Gross Margin	Operating Margin	Profit Margin
50.63	17.14	4.62

Growth Rates (%)

Sales	1 year	23.08	3 years	23.06	5 years	14.20
EPS	1 year	115.19	3 years	16.74	5 years	2.87

Miller's assessment of Mandalay Resorts:

Miller bought this stock too early, expecting an early turnaround in Las Vegas after the overbuilding in the mid-1990s. He kept buying as the share price declined. Three years after the first purchases, the share price tripled.

Figure 15   Mattel Inc.

Market Cap: $7,837,250,000

Revenue (2001 through July): $1,586,248,000

Mattel, Inc. designs, manufactures, markets and distributes a variety of family products on a worldwide basis. These are sold under such well known names as Barbie, Fisher-Price, Hot Wheels and Tyco products.

Stock History

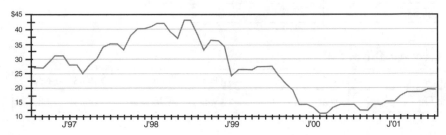

Key Ratios and Statistics

Valuation (ratios)

Price/Earnings	Price/Sales	Price/Book	Price/Cash Flow
39.80	1.72	5.55	17.32

Per Share ($)

Earnings	Sales	Book	Cash Flow	Cash	Return/ Equity	Return/ Assets	Return/ Investment
0.46	10.60	3.28	1.05	0.17	13.55	4.33	7.07

Profitability (%, 12 months to June 2001)

Gross Margin	Operating Margin	Profit Margin
44.89	5.48	4.15

Growth Rates (%)

Sales	1 year 1.62	3 years −5.05	5 years 1.34
EPS	1 year 61.79	3 years	5 years −18.53

Miller's assessment of Mattel:

Mattel presented an opportunity based on a depressed share price. Mattel has a line of products and a name brand that can survive management and marketing problems.

Figure 16   MCI/Worldcom (NASDAQ—MCIT)

Market Cap: $2,070,980,000

Revenue (2001 through July): $7,170,000,000

Traded as one of Worldcom's two tracking stocks, MCI includes Worldcom's consumer operations. MCI provides a broad range of communications services including long-distance voice communications, consumer local voice communications, wireless messaging, private line services, and dial-up internet access. MCI had 27,100 employees at the end of 2001.

Stock History

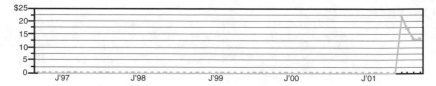

Key Ratios and Statistics

Valuation (ratios)

Price/Earnings	Price/Sales	Price/Book	Price/Cash Flow
3.53	0.12	0.69	1.22

Per Share ($)

Earnings	Sales	Book	Cash Flow	Cash	Return/ Equity	Return/ Assets	Return/ Investment
4.24	128.74	21.65	12.21	0.23	20.36	3.53	5.04

Profitability (%, 12 months to July 2001)

Gross Margin	Operating Margin	Profit Margin
51.94	8.98	3.37

Growth Rates (%)

Sales	1 year	1.01	3 years	N/A	5 years	N/A
EPS	1 year	−4.98	3 years	N/A	5 years	N/A

Miller's assessment of MCI:

He spotted this company as an up-and-coming leader in the changing telecommunications environment. It seemed undervalued in terms of its potential and became a core holding in 1990. Miller retained his holding when Worldcom acquired MCI in 1998, but he sold the position at the beginning of 2001. (Miller sold his MCI Worldcom before it split into two tracking stocks, including the one described above.)

Figure 17   Microsoft Corporation (NASDAQ—MSFT)

Market Cap: $333,959,430,000

Revenue (Fiscal 2001) $25,296,000,000

Microsoft Corporation develops, manufactures, licenses, and supports a range of software products, including operating systems, server applications, Internet browsers, worker productivity applications, and software development tools. As of June 2000, Microsoft had 39,100 employees.

Stock History

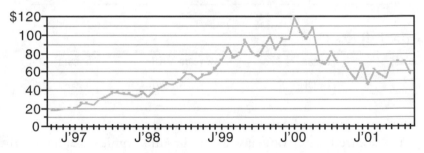

Key Ratios and Statistics

Valuation (ratios)

Price/Earnings	Price/Sales	Price/Book	Price/Cash Flow
44.67	13.67	7.06	44.80

Per Share ($)

Earnings	Sales	Book	Cash Flow	Cash	Return/ Equity	Return/ Assets	Return/ Investment
1.39	4.54	8.79	1.39	5.87	16.89	13.56	16.41

Profitability (%, 12 months to August 2001)

Gross Margin	Operating Margin	Profit Margin
86.34	46.33	30.52

Growth Rates (%)

Sales	1 year	10.19	3 years	18.34	5 years	22.82
EPS	1 year	−18.48	3 years	18.52	5 years	26.42

Miller's assessment of Microsoft:

He didn't buy this debt free growth stock, but wished he had Microsoft always looks priccy to those who don't understand the principles of increasing returns.

Figure 18   Nextel Communications, Inc. (NASDAQ—NXTL)

Market Cap: $9,730,040,000

Revenue (2001 through July): $3,623,000,000

Nextel provides a wide array of digital wireless communications services utilizing a single transmission technology to customers throughout the United States. Already providing business users with wireless phone service, two-way radio dispatch, paging, and text messaging on one handset, Nextel has added wireless Internet access and international roaming. As of the end of 2000, Nextel had 19,500 employees.

Stock History

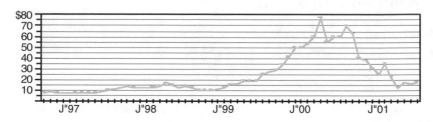

Appendix 4   Charts

Key Ratios and Statistics

Valuation (ratios)

Price/Earnings	Price/Sales	Price/Book	Price/Cash Flow
N/A	1.41	12.96	11.49

Per Share ($)

Earnings	Sales	Book	Cash Flow	Cash	Return/ Equity	Return/ Assets	Return/ Investment
−1.51	8.91	0.97	1.09	6.18	−74.96	−4.15	−4.65

Profitability (%, 12 months to July 2001)

Gross Margin	Operating Margin	Profit Margin
61.87	−0.18	−13.71

Growth Rates (%)

Sales	1 year 50.92	3 years 97.74	5 years 101.50
EPS	N/A	N/A	N/A

Miller's assessment of Nextel:

The company is attractive because it has the highest average revenue per unit in its industry, and is well differentiated from Sprint and AT&T Wireless.

Figure 19   Nokia Corporation (NYSE—NOK)

Market Cap: $99,623,890,000

Revenue (2001 through July): $13,971,000,000

Nokia is a supplier of telecommunications systems and equipment. The company's core businesses include the development, manufacture, and delivery of mobile phones, and mobile, fixed, and IP networks.

Stock History

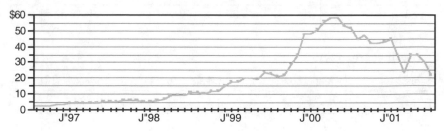

Key Ratios and Statistics

Valuation (ratios)

Price/Earnings	Price/Sales	Price/Book	Price/Cash Flow
31.74	3.60	10.36	24.17

Per Share ($)

Earnings	Sales	Book	Cash Flow	Cash	Return/ Equity	Return/ Assets	Return/ Investment
0.67	5.88	2.05	0.88	0.78	36.51	19.66	36.00

Profitability (%, 12 months to July 2001)

Gross Margin	Operating Margin	Profit Margin
36.32	16.37	11.78

Growth Rates (%)

Sales	1 year	53.63	3 years	50.85	5 years	37.45
EPS	1 year	49.90	3 years	52.15	5 years	41.21

Miller's assessment of Nokia:

He made an early (1995) investment in a great business—one that redefined the way the telephone is used.

Figure 20   Philip Morris Companies (NYSE—MO)

Market Cap: $94,937,330,000

Revenue (2001 through July): $45,547,000,000

Philip Morris is a holding company whose principal subsidiaries are engaged in the manufacture and sale of various consumer products, including cigarettes, packaged and processed foods, and beverages.

Stock History

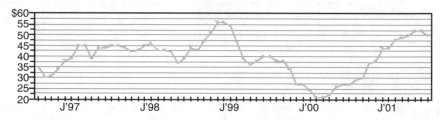

Key Ratios and Statistics

Valuation (ratios)

Price/Earnings	Price/Sales	Price/Book	Price/Cash Flow
11.48	1.13	4.84	10.42

Per Share ($)

Earnings	Sales	Book	Cash Flow	Cash	Return/ Equity	Return/ Assets	Return/ Investment
3.76	38.05	8.92	4.14	0.18	52.96	11.73	17.30

Profitability (%, 12 months to July 2001)

Gross Margin	Operating Margin	Profit Margin
43.44	17.85	9.89

Growth Rates (%)

Sales	1 year	2.24	3 years	3.70	5 years	3.99
EPS	1 year	17.28	3 years	13.18	5 years	11.66

Miller's assessment of Philip Morris:

Many value investors wanted to buy this stock, but were reluctant to buy tobacco stocks. Philip Morris management had mitigated against tobacco company lawsuits, but when Miller bought in the early 1990s, the share priced suffered from legal difficulties, anyway.

Figure 21   R. J. Reynolds Tobacco (NYSE—RJR)

Market Cap: $5,097,770,000

Revenue (2001 through July): $4,219,000,000

R.J. Reynolds Tobacco Holdings is a holding company for Reynolds Tobacco, the second largest cigarette manufacturer in the United States, whose major brands include Doral, Winston, Camel, Salem, and Vantage. The company has 8,100 employees.

Stock History

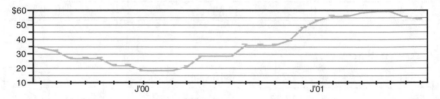

Key Ratios and Statistics

Valuation (ratios)

Price/Earnings	Price/Sales	Price/Book	Price/Cash Flow
13.05	0.61	0.61	5.95

Per Share ($)

Earnings	Sales	Book	Cash Flow	Cash	Return/ Equity	Return/ Assets	Return/ Investment
3.85	82.89	83.00	8.45	24.57	5.05	2.59	3.26

Profitability (%, 12 months to July 2001)

Gross Margin	Operating Margin	Profit Margin
59.38	10.08	4.65

Growth Rates (%)

Sales	1 year 7.93	3 years 17.43	5 years 14.80
EPS	1 year 92.43	3 years 170.30	5 years 13.51

Miller's assessment:

Called RJR Nabisco when Miller owned it, it was a company with good financial figures, but beaten up by external factors. Miller bought RJR in 1991 and held until 1997.

Figure 22   Symantec Corporation (NASDAQ—SYMC)

Market Cap: $3,080,570,000

Revenue (Fiscal 2001): $853,000,000

Symantec is a world leader in Internet security technology and provides a broad range of content and network security solutions to individuals and businesses. Symantec makes security (Norton AntiVirus), desktop efficiency (Norton CleanSweep), and PC utility (Norton Ghost) software products. It also offers software that lets PC users work from remote locations. As of March 2001, Symantec had 3,800 employees.

Stock History

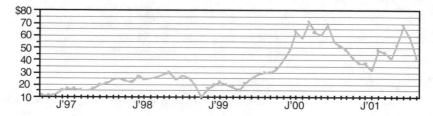

Key Ratios and Statistics

Valuation (ratios)

Price/Earnings	Price/Sales	Price/Book	Price/Cash Flow
253.94	3.26	2.17	16.60

Per Share ($)

Earnings	Sales	Book	Cash Flow	Cash	Return/ Equity	Return/ Assets	Return/ Investment
0.17	12.85	19.33	2.52	8.48	0.37	0.29	0.37

Profitability (%, 12 months to August 2001)

Gross Margin	Operating Margin	Profit Margin
84.48	4.84	0.49

Growth Rates (%)

Sales	1 year	14.46	3 years	17.00	5 years	13.89
EPS	1 year	−65.74	3 years	−13.00	5 years	18.83

Miller's assessment of Symantec:

Good position in a powerful, important market and good management. The company had a low multiple and fast top-line growth and generates a lot of cash.

Figure 23   Toys "R" Us, Inc. (NYSE—TOY)

Market Cap: $4,936,430,000

Revenue (2001 through July): $4,082,000,000

Toys "R" Us is a retailer of children's products through 1,201 toy stores, 198 Kids "R" Us children's clothing stores, 145 Babies "R" Us infant stores, and 37 Imaginarium educational specialty stores. The company offers toys, games, sporting goods, electronics, software, kids' apparel and furniture at these stores. As of February 2001, the company had 69,000 employees.

Stock History

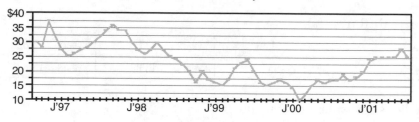

Key Ratios and Statistics

Valuation (ratios)

Price/Earnings	Price/Sales	Price/Book	Price/Cash Flow
37.50	0.45	1.45	11.09

Per Share ($)

Earnings	Sales	Book	Cash Flow	Cash	Return/ Equity	Return/ Assets	Return/ Investment
0.66	55.62	17.13	2.25	1.47	4.15	1.69	2.61

Profitability (%, 12 months to July 2001)

Gross Margin	Operating Margin	Profit Margin
31.28	3.44	1.25

Growth Rates (%)

Sales	1 year −4.47	3 years 0.88	5 years 3.75
EPS	1 year 65.26	3 years 3.41	5 years 28.56

Miller's assessment of Toys "R" Us:

This became an unpopular name, but it has a strong name recognition. Miller had faith in the company's ventures into other children's lines, and the stock indeed became a winner.

Figure 24   Waste Management Inc. (NYSE—WMI)

Market Cap: $18,940,000,000

Revenue (2001 through July): $2,719,000,000

Waste Management Inc. provides integrated waste management services consisting of collection, transfer, disposal, recycling, and resource recovery services as well as other hazardous waste services to commercial, industrial, municipal, and residential customers. In 1998, USA Waste bought Waste Management, taking its name. As of the end of the year 2000, Waste Management had 57,000 employees.

Stock History

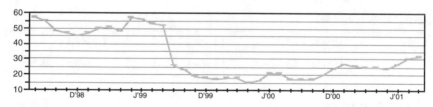

Key Ratios and Statistics

Valuation (ratios)

Price/Earnings	Price/Sales	Price/Book	Price/Cash Flow
	1.58	3.84	13.66

Per Share ($)

Earnings	Sales	Book	Cash Flow	Cash	Return/ Equity	Return/ Assets	Return/ Investment
−0.05	19.21	7.89	2.22	1.42	−0.62	−0.15	−0.19

Profitability (%, 12 months to July 2001)

Gross Margin	Operating Margin	Profit Margin
39.74	8.81	−0.24

Growth Rates (%)

Sales	1 year −4.84	3 years 1.43	5 years 59.34

Miller's assessment of Waste Management:

This had been the quintessential growth stock in the 1980s, but there were management problems and consolidation in the industry. Its share price fell drastically after a 1999 accounting scandal. It had an irresistible multiple and accelerating free cash flow.

Figure 25   WPP Group plc (NASDAQ—WPPGY)

Market Cap: $11,158,580,000

Revenue (2001 through July): $ 4,769,120,000

WPP Group plc provides national and international communications services such as advertising, media planning, buying and research, information and consultancy, public relations and affairs, and specialist communications. WPP Group is the world's number 2 advertising and media services conglomerate. WPP Group had 51,195 employees at the end of 2001.

Stock History

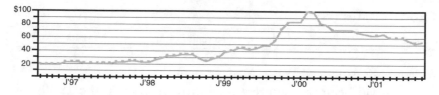

Key Ratios and Statistics

Valuation (ratios)

Price/Earnings	Price/Sales	Price/Book	Price/Cash Flow
25.33	2.05	2.30	18.21

Per Share ($)

Earnings	Sales	Book	Cash Flow	Cash	Return/ Equity	Return/ Assets	Return/ Investment
1.98	24.53	21.86	2.76	6.84	17.77	4.81	10.72

Profitability (%, 12 months to July 2001)

Gross Margin	Operating Margin	Profit Margin
91.79	13.96	8.59

Growth Rates (%)

Sales	1 year	37.20	3 years	19.50	5 years	13.90
EPS	1 year	31.80	3 years	2.75	5 years	32.14

Miller's assessment of WPP:

This was a classic value special situation, or turnaround. When the turnaround came, it came quickly.

NOTES

INTRODUCTION

1. Diane Banegas, "Mutual Fund Manager Bill Miller Sees Value in Business Network," *Santa Fe Institute Bulletin*, Winter 1998.

2. Karen Damato and Aaron Lucchetti, "Bull Run: Mr. Miller of Legg Mason Will Beat S&P 500 for 9th Year in a Row," *Wall Street Journal*, December 31, 1999.

CHAPTER 1

1. Patrick McGeehan, "A Manager's Fight to Keep a Streak Alive," *New York Times*, January 7, 2001.

2. Tom Abate, "Some Recommended Reading for the Serious High Tech Player," *San Francisco Chronicle*, October 24, 1998.

3. Mary Rowland, "Is There Still Value in Value Funds," *MoneyCentral Investor*, MSN.com, April 7, 1999.

4. Jeffrey M. Laderman, "Value Investors Learn New Tricks," www.businessweek.com, June 14, 1999.

5. "Shopping for Value," *USAA Financial Spectrum*, Fall, 2001.

6. Michael Santoli, "Best Sometimes Are Brightest," Barron's Online, April 2, 2001.

7. "Legg Mason Opportunity," *Kiplinger's Magazine*, March 2000.

8. Landon Thomas Sr., "Miller's Crossing," *Smart Money*, July 2000, p. 126.

9. Patrick McGeehan, "A Manager's Fight to Keep a Streak Alive," *New York Times*, January 7, 2001.

10. Ibid.

11. "World of Value in Key Stocks," CNNfn, June 19, 2000, http://cnnfn. cnn.com.

12. Ed McCarthy, "Bill Miller, Portfolio Manager of Legg Mason Value Trust, Has Beaten the S&P 500 Index Eight Years in a Row," Money-live chat, www.money.com, October 6, 1999.

13. Adam Shell, "Funds & Personal Finance," *Investor's Business Daily*, November 26, 1999.

14. Ibid.

15. Ed McCarthy, "Bill Miller, Portfolio Manager of Legg Mason Value Trust, Has Beaten the S&P 500 Index Eight Years in a Row," Money-live chat, www.money.com, October 6, 1999.

16. "To Beat the Market: Hire a Philosopher," *New York Times*, September 3, 1999.

17. Mark Culloton, "What a Contrarian Buys in a Richly Valued Market," Morningstar.com, June 9, 2000.

18. Ibid.

19. "The Pabrai Investment Fund I (PIFI) Announces 62.5 Percent Returns in First Year," *Business Wire*, July 26, 2000.

20. Legg Mason Value Trust Inc., *Fund Update*, March 31, 2001.

21. Tom Lauricella, "Oakmark Select Funds to Stop Accepting New Investors," *Wall Street Journal*, April 25, 2001.

22. Legg Mason Value Trust Inc., *Fund Update*, March 31, 2001.

23. Jeffrey M. Laderman, "Value Investors Learn New Tricks," www.businessweek.com, June 14, 1999.

24. "Legg Mason Opportunity Trust," *Kiplinger's Magazine*, March 2000.

25. Ed McCarthy, "Bill Miller, Portfolio Manager of Legg Mason Value Trust, Has Beaten the S&P 500 Index Eight Years in a Row," Money-live chat, www.money.com, October 6, 1999.

26. Karen Damato and Aaron Lucchetti, "Bull Run: Mr. Miller of Legg Mason Will Beat S&P 500 for 9th Year in a Row," *Wall Street Journal*, December 31, 1999.

27. Ibid.

28. Ibid.

29. Ibid.

30. Author interview with Ernie Kiehne, July 24, 2001, Baltimore, Maryland.

31. William H. Miller III, *Legg Mason Value Trust Annual Report*, March 31, 1993.

32. Ibid.

33. Ibid.

34. Karen Damato and Aaron Lucchetti, "Bull Run: Mr. Miller of Legg Mason Will Beat S&P 500 for 9th Year in a Row," *Wall Street Journal*, December 31, 1999.

35. William H. Miller III, *Legg Mason Value Trust Annual Report*, March 31, 1994.

36. Karen Damato and Aaron Lucchetti, "Bull Run: Mr. Miller of Legg Mason Will Beat S&P 500 for 9th Year in a Row," *Wall Street Journal*, December 31, 1999.

37. Ibid.

38. Ibid.

39. William H. Miller III, *Legg Mason Value Trust Inc., Special Investment Trust Inc., and Total Return Trust Inc. Annual Report*, March 31, 1997.

40. Ibid.

41. Karen Damato and Aaron Lucchetti, "Bull Run: Mr. Miller of Legg Mason Will Beat S&P 500 for 9th Year in a Row," *Wall Street Journal*, December 31, 1999.

42. Ibid.

43. Patrick McGeehan, "A Manager's Fight to Keep a Streak Alive," *New York Times,* January 7, 2001.

44. Ibid.

45. Bill Miller letter, *Legg Mason Value Trust Annual Report,* January 2001.

46. Joe Bousquin, "Legg Mason's Miller to Launch Go-Anywhere Fund," TheStreet.com, October 21, 1999.

47. Landon Thomas Sr., "Miller's Crossing," *Smart Money,* July 2000, p. 126.

48. Karen Damato and Aaron Lucchetti, "Bull Run: Mr. Miller of Legg Mason Will Beat S&P 500 for 9th Year in a Row," *Wall Street Journal,* December 31, 1999.

49. Author interview with Brian Arthur, Santa Fe Institute, Santa Fe, New Mexico, May 10, 2001.

CHAPTER 2

1. Karen Damato and Aaron Lucchetti, "Bull Run: Mr. Miller of Legg Mason Will Beat S&P 500 for 9th Year in a Row," *Wall Street Journal,* December 31, 1999.

2. Ibid.

3. Robert Hagstrom, *Latticework: The New Investing* (New York: Texere, 2000), p 10.

4. Kirk Kazanjian, *Wizards of Wall Street* (New York: New York Institute of Finance, 2000).

5. Robert Hagstrom, *Latticework: The New Investing* (New York: Texere, 2000), p. 134.

6. Robert Hagstrom, *Latticework: The New Investing* (New York: Texere, 2000), p. 134.

7. Karen Damato and Aaron Lucchetti, "Bull Run: Mr. Miller of Legg

Mason Will Beat S&P 500 for 9th Year in a Row," *Wall Street Journal*, December 31, 1999.

8. W. Brian Arthur, "The End of Certainty in Economics," Talk given at the Conference *Einstein Meets Magritte*, Free University of Brussels, July 1994.

9. Ibid.

10. W. Brian Arthur, Steven Durlauf, and David A. Lane, *The Economy as an Evolving Complex System II* (Reading, Mass.: Addison-Wesley, 1997), Introduction.

11. Ibid.

12. Bertrand Ducharme, "Algorithms Inspired by Social Insects," book review, www.amazon.com, February 13, 2000.

13. Eric Bonabeau, "Swarm Intelligence Takes Over," www.futureof software.nct, Winter 2000–2001.

14. Ibid.

15. Jesper Hoffmeyer, "The Swarm Body," www.olbio.ku.dk.

16. W. Brian Arthur, *Increasing Returns and Path Dependence in the Economy* (University of Michigan Press, 1994), Preface, p. 2.

17. Ibid.

18. Joel Kurtzman, "An Interview with W. Brian Arthur," http://www. strategybusiness.com/thoughtleaders/98209/page1.html.

19. W. Brian Arthur, "Positive Feedback in the Economy," *Scientific American*, 262, 92–99, Feb. 1990.

20. Joel Kurtzman, "An Interview with W. Brian Arthur," http://www. strategybusiness.com/thoughtleaders/98209/page1.html.

21. W. Brian Arthur, "Positive Feedback in the Economy," *Scientific American*, 262, 92–99, Feb. 1990.

22. W. Brian Arthur, "Positive Feedback in the Economy," *Scientific American*, 262, 92–99, Feb. 1990.

23. Dominic Gates, "The Pretext Interview," www.pretext.com/ May98/columns/intview.htm. W. Brian Arthur, "Increasing Returns

and the New World of Business," *Harvard Business Review*, July–August 1996.

24. W. Brian Arthur, "Positive Feedback in the Economy," *Scientific American*, 262, 92–99, Feb. 1990.

25. W. Brian Arthur, "Competing Technologies, Increasing Returns, and Lock-in by Historical Events," First appeared in IIASA Paper WP-83-90, September 1983. Published in *Economic Journal*, 99, 116–131, 1989.

26. Joel Kurtzman, "An Interview with W. Brian Arthur," http://www.strategybusiness.com/thoughtleaders/98902/page1.html.

27. W. Brian Arthur, "Competing Technologies, Increasing Returns, and Lock-in by Historical Events," First appeared in IIASA Paper WP-83-90, September 1983. Published in *Economic Journal*, 99, 116–131, 1989.

28. Dominic Gates, "The Pretext Interview," http://www.pretext.com/May98/columns/interview.htm.

29. Joel Kurtzman, "An Interview with W. Brian Arthur," http://www.strategybusiness.com/thoughtleaders/98209/page1.html.

30. W. Brian Arthur, *Increasing Returns and Path Dependence in the Economy* (Ann Arbor: University of Michigan Press, 1994), Preface, p. 2.

31. Joel Kurtzman, "An Interview with W. Brian Arthur," http://www.strategybusiness.com/thoughtleaders/98209/page1.html.

32. Dominic Gates, "The Pretext Interview," http://www.pretext.com/May98/columns/interview.htm.

33. Hal R. Varian, "The Information Economy," *Scientific American*, 200–201, September 1995.

34. Joel Kurtzman, "An Interview with W. Brian Arthur," http://www.strategybusiness.com/thoughtleaders/98209/page1.html.

35. Ibid.

36. Bill Miller letter, *Legg Mason Value Trust Annual Report*, January 2001.

37. Ibid.

38. Joel Kurtzman, "An Interview with W. Brian Arthur," http://www.strategybusiness.com/thoughtleaders/98209/page1.html.

39. Ibid.

40. Ibid.

41. Ibid.

42. Ibid.

43. Ibid.

44. W. Brian Arthur, "Inductive Reasoning and Bounded Reality (The El Farol Problem)," Paper given at the American Economic Association Annual Meetings, 1994. Published in *American Economic Review* (Papers and Proceedings), 84, 106–111, 1994.

45. Kirk Kazanjian, *Wizard of Wall Street* (New York: New York Institute of Finance, 2000).

46. Robert Hagstrom, *Latticework: The New Investing* (New York: Texere, 2000), p. 64.

CHAPTER 3

1. William H. Miller III, *Legg Mason Value Trust Inc., Special Investment Trust Inc., and Total Return Trust Inc. Annual Report*, March 31, 1997.

2. Mark Niemann, interview with author, December, 2001.

3. Jeffrey M. Laderman, "Value Investors Learn New Tricks," www.businessweek.com, June 14, 1999.

4. Kirk Kazanjian, *Wizards of Wall Street* (New York: New York Institute of Finance, 2000).

5. Adam Shell, "Funds & Personal Finance," *Investor's Business Daily*, November 26, 1999.

6. Richard C. Ten Wolde, "Most Valuable Player," *Barron's Online*, January 11, 1999.

7. Janet Lowe, interview with Bill Miller.

8. Ibid.

9. "Legg Mason Opportunity," *Kiplinger's Magazine*, March, 2000.

10. David Henry, "The Numbers Game," *Business Week*, May 14, 2001, p. 100.

11. "Time to Cut the Accounting Shenanigans," *Business Week*, May 14, 2001, p. 146.

12. John Burr Williams, *The Theory of Investment Value* (Burlington, Vt.: Fraser Books, 1997), Preface.

13. Ibid.

14. Ibid.

15. Ibid.

16. Carol Marie Cropper, "Taking the Measure of a Stock," *Business Week*, May 14, 2001, p. 123.

17. Adam Shell, "Funds & Personal Finance," *Investor's Business Daily*, November 26, 1999.

18. Sandra Ward, "Underpriced Market," *Barron's Online*, April 9, 2001.

19. William H. Miller III, *Legg Mason Value Trust Inc., Special Investment Trust Inc., and Total Return Trust Inc. Annual Report*, March 31, 2000.

20. Ed McCarthy, "Bill Miller, Portfolio Manager of Legg Mason Value Trust, Has Beaten the S&P 500 Index Eight Years in a Row," Money-live chat, www.money.com, October 6, 1999.

21. Ibid.

22. Kirk Kazanjian, *Wizards of Wall Street* (New York: New York Institute of Finance, 2000).

23. Adam Shell, "Funds & Personal Finance," *Investor's Business Daily*, November 26, 1999.

24. William H. Miller III, *Legg Mason Value Trust Inc., Special Investment Trust Inc., and Total Return Trust Inc. Annual Report*, March 31, 1998.

25. Robert G. Hagstrom, *Latticework: The New Investing* (New York: Texere, 2001), p. 137.

26. Kirk Kazanjian, *Wizards of Wall Street* (New York: New York Institute of Finance, 2000).

27. Ibid.

28. Ibid.

29. Ed McCarthy, "Bill Miller, Portfolio Manager of Legg Mason Value Trust, Has Beaten the S&P 500 Index Eight Years in a Row," Money-live chat, www.money.com, October 6, 1999.

30. Ibid.

31. Jeffrey M. Laderman, "Value Investors Learn New Tricks," www.businessweek.com, June 14, 1999.

32. Bill Miller, interview with author, July, 2001.

33. Kirk Kazanjian, *Wizards of Wall Street* (New York: New York Institute of Finance, 2000).

34. William H. Miller III, *Legg Mason Value Trust Inc., Special Investment Trust Inc., and Total Return Trust Inc. Annual Report*, March 31, 2000.

35. Adam Shell, "Funds & Personal Finance," *Investor's Business Daily*, November 26, 1999.

36. William H. Miller III, *Legg Mason Value Trust Annual Report*, March 31, 1995.

37. Ibid.

38. Ibid.

39. Ibid.

40. Adam Shell, "Funds & Personal Finance," *Investor's Business Daily*, November 26, 1999.

41. Karen Damato and Aaron Lucchetti, "Bull Run: Mr. Miller of Legg Mason Will Beat S&P 500 for 9th Year in a Row," *Wall Street Journal*, December 31, 1999.

CHAPTER 4

1. William H. Miller III, *Legg Mason Value Trust Annual Report*, March 31, 1990.

2. Ibid.

3. Kirk Kazanjian, *Wizards of Wall Street* (New York: New York Institute of Finance, 2000).

4. William H. Miller, *Legg Mason Value Trust Annual Report*, March 31, 1995.

5. Kirk Kazanjian, *Wizards of Wall Street* (New York: New York Institute of Finance, 2000).

6. Ibid.

7. Patrick McGeehan, "A Manager's Fight to Keep a Streak Alive," *New York Times*, January 7, 2001.

8. Kirk Kazanjian, *Wizards of Wall Street* (New York: New York Institute of Finance, 2000).

9. Ibid.

10. Timothy Middleton, "Don't Let the 'Value' Label Fool You," *MSN Money*, February 2, 1999.

11. Karen Damato and Aaron Lucchelli, "Bull Run: Mr. Miller of Legg Mason Will Beat S&P 500 for 9th Year in a Row," *Wall Street Journal*, December 31, 1999.

12. Ibid.

13. Ibid.

14. Ibid.

15. Ibid.

16. Kirk Kazanjian, *Wizards of Wall Street* (New York: New York Institute of Finance, 2000).

17. Ibid.

18. Ibid.

19. William H. Miller III, *Legg Mason Value Trust Annual Report*, March 31, 1992.

20. Ibid.

21. Ibid.

22. Ibid.

23. Ibid.

24. "Value Preachers Spread the Gospel," *Fundsnet Insight*, Volume 8, Number 5, May 2001, p. 10.

25. Ibid.

26. Kirk Kazanjian, *Wizards of Wall Street* (New York: New York Institute of Finance, 2000).

27. William H. Miller III, *Legg Mason Value Trust Annual Report*, March 31, 1992.

28. Timothy Middleton, "Don't Let the 'Value' Label Fool You," *MSN Money*, February 2, 1999.

29. Kirk Kazanjian, *Wizards of Wall Street* (New York: New York Institute of Finance, 2000).

30. Ibid.

CHAPTER 5

1. Patrick McGeehan, "A Manager's Fight to Keep a Streak Alive," *New York Times,* January 7, 2001.

2. Gretchen Morgenson, "Analyze This," New York Times News Service, *San Diego Union-Tribune,* March 20, 2001, p. C1.

3. Mary Rowland, "Is There Still Value in Value Funds," *MoneyCentral Investor,* MSN.com, April 7, 1999.

4. Ibid.

5. Bill Miller letter, *Legg Mason Value Trust Annual Report,* January 2001.

6. Ibid.

7. Bill Miller, interview with author, Baltimore, Maryland July, 2001.

8. To Beat the Market: Hire a Philosopher," *New York Times,* September 3, 1999.

9. W. Brian Arthur, "Increasing Returns and the New World of Business," *Harvard Business Review,* July–August 1996.

10. Ibid.

11. Ibid.

12. Ibid.

13. W. Brian Arthur, "Positive Feedback in the Economy," *Scientific American,* February 1990, pp. 92–99.

14. Lauren Martin, "The Anti-Guru Information Guru," *Sydney Morning Herald,* June 4, 1999.

15. Ibid.

16. Ibid.

17. "Building a Road Map for the Network Economy: A Conversation with Carl Shapiro and Hal R. Varian." www.hbsp.harvard.edu/ideasatwork.

18. Hal R. Varian, "The Information Economy," *Scientific American,* September 1995, pp. 200–201.

19. Hal R. Varian and Carl Shapiro, *Information Rules: A Strategic Guide to the Network Economy* (Cambridge: Harvard Business School Press, 1998).

20. Lauren Martin, "The Anti-Guru Information Guru," *Sydney Morning Herald,* June 4, 1999.

21. Hal R. Varian, "Economics and Search," www.sims.berkeley.edu.

22. Joel Kurtzman, "An Interview with W. Brian Arthur," http://www.strategy-business.com/thoughtleaders/98209/pagel.html.

23. "Legg Mason Opportunity," *Kiplinger's Magazine,* March, 2000.

24. Richard C. Ten Wolde, "Most Valuable Player," *Barron's Online,* January 11, 1999.

25. William H. Miller, *Legg Mason Value Trust Annual Report,* March 31, 1993.

26. Bill Miller, author interview, Baltimore Maryland, July 2001.

27. Ibid.

28. Ibid.

29. Ibid.

30. Ibid.

31. William H. Miller, *Legg Mason Value Trust Annual Report,* March 31, 1993.

32. William H. Miller, *Legg Mason Value Trust Annual Report,* March 31, 1994.

33. Karen Damato and Aaron Lucchetti, "Bull Run: Mr. Miller of Legg Mason Will Beat S&P 500 for 9th Year in a Row," *Wall Street Journal,* December 31, 1999.

34. Letters to the Editor, Robert A. Hauslen, *Barron's,* April 23, 2001.

35. Letters to the Editor, Carl Riley, *Barron's,* April 23, 2001.

36. Adam Shell, "Funds & Personal Finance," *Investor's Business Daily,* November 26, 1999.

37. Ibid.

38. Landon Thomas Sr., "Miller's Crossing," *Smart Money,* July 2000, p. 126.

39. Ed McCarthy, "Bill Miller, Portfolio Manager of Legg Mason Value Trust, Has Beaten the S&P 500 Index Eight Years in a Row," Money-live chat, www.money.com, October 6, 1999.

40. Jeffrey M. Laderman, "Value Investors Learn New Tricks," www.businessweek.com, June 14, 1999.

41. Sandra Ward, "Underpriced Market," *Barron's Online,* April 9, 2001.

42. Ibid.

43. Ibid.

44. Nick Wingfield, "Amazon.com's 'M-Commerce' Effort Fizzles Along with the Wireless Web," *Wall Street Journal,* May 7, 2001, p. B1.

45. "Ashford Probe Seen Tied to Amazon," CBS.MarketWatch.com, August 25, 2001.

46. David Henry, "The Number's Game," *Business Week,* May 14, 2001, p. 102.

47. Ibid.

48. Sandra Ward, "Underpriced Market," *Barron's Online,* April 9, 2001.

49. "World of Value in Key Stocks," CNNfn, June 19, 2000, http://cnn fn.cnn.com.

50. Sandra Ward, "Underpriced Market," *Barron's Online,* April 9, 2001.

51. "Legg Mason Opportunity," *Kiplinger's Magazine,* March 2000.

52. Sandra Ward, "Land of Obscurity," *Barron's Online,* April 30, 2001.

53. Patrick McGeehan, "A Manager's Fight to Keep a Streak Alive," *New York Times,* January 7, 2001.

54. Timothy Middleton, "Don't Let the 'Value' Label Fool You," *MSN Money,* February 2, 1999.

55. Ed McCarthy, "Bill Miller, Portfolio Manager of Legg Mason Value Trust, Has Beaten the S&P 500 Index Eight Years in a Row," Money-live chat, www.money.com, October 6, 1999.

56. "Legg Mason Opportunity," *Kiplinger's Magazine,* March 2000.

57. Ibid.

58. "To Beat the Market: Hire a Philosopher," *New York Times,* September 3, 1999.

59. Ibid.

60. William Green, "It's Bill Miller Time," *Fortune,* December 10, 2001, p. 154.

61. David Henry, "The Number's Game," *Business Week,* May 14, 2001, p. 102.

62. Mary Rowland, "Is There Still Value in Value Funds," *MoneyCentral Investor,* MSN.com, April 7, 1999.

63. "Value Investors Learn New Tricks," www.businessweek.com, June 14, 1999.

64. Landon Thomas Sr., "Miller's Crossing," *SmartMoney,* July 2000, p. 126.

65. Janet Lowe, Interview with Bill Miller.

66. Sandra Ward, "Underpriced Market," *Barron's Online,* April 9, 2001.

67. Ibid.

68. Adam Shell, "Funds & Personal Finance," *Investor's Business Daily,* November 26, 1999.

69. Jeffrey M. Laderman, "Value Investors Learn New Tricks," www.businessweek.com June 14, 1999.

70. Ibid.

71. Landon Thomas Sr., "Miller's Crossing," *SmartMoney,* July 2000, p. 126.

72. Ibid.

73. Ibid.

74. Gretchen Morgenson, "Analyze This," New York Times News Service, *San Diego-Union Tribune,* March 20, 2001, p. C1.

75. "Market Commentary from Portfolio Manager Bill Miller, from Remarks Made April 20, 2000," www.LeggMason.com.

76. Legg Mason Value Trust Inc., *Fund Update,* March 31, 2001.

77. Ibid.

78. Gretchen Morgenson, "Analyze This," New York Times News Service, *San Diego-Union Tribune,* March 20, 2001, p. C1.

79. Kristi E. Swartz, "Is Tech Dead?" *Business Journalist*, August/September 2001.

80. W. Brian Arthur, "Increasing Returns and the New World of Business," *Harvard Business Review*, July–August 1996.

81. Hal R. Varian, "Boolean Trades and Hurricane Bonds," *Wall Street Journal Interactive Edition*, May 8, 2000.

CHAPTER 6

1. Paul Krugman, "The Web Gets Ugly," *New York Times Magazine*, December 6, 1998.

2. John Cassidy, "The Force of an Idea," *New Yorker*, January 12, 1998, p. 32.

3. Hal R. Varian, "The Information Economy," *Scientific American*, September 1995, pp. 200–201.

4. Ibid.

5. "Building a Road Map for the Network Economy: A Conversation with Carl Shapiro and Hal R. Varian," www.hbsp.harvard.edu/ideasatwork.

6. Ibid.

7. W. Brian Arthur, "Increasing Returns and the New World of Business," *Harvard Business Review*, July–August 1996.

8. W. Brian Arthur, interview with author, Santa Fe, New Mexico, May, 2001.

9. W. Brian Arthur, "Increasing Returns and the New World of Business," *Harvard Business Review*, July–August 1996.

10. Ibid.

11. Ibid.

12. Ibid.

13. W. Brian Arthur, "Appraising Microsoft and Its Global Strategy," Handout for the Ralph Nader Conference, Washington, D.C., November 13, 1997.

Notes

CHAPTER 7

1. "To Beat the Market: Hire a Philosopher," *New York Times*, September 3, 1999.

2. William H Miller III, *Legg Mason Value Trust Annual Report*, March 31, 1996.

3. Bill Miller letter, *Legg Mason Value Trust Annual Report*, January, 2001.

4. W. Brian Arthur, "Increasing Returns and the New World of Business," *Harvard Business Review*, July–August 1996.

5. W. Brian Arthur, Steven Durlauf, and David A. Lane, *The Economy as an Evolving Complex System II* (Reading, Mass.: Addison-Wesley, 1997).

6. Patrick McGeehan, "A Manager's Fight to Keep a Streak Alive," *New York Times*, January 7, 2001.

7. Bill Miller letter, *Legg Mason Value Trust Annual Report*, January, 2001.

8. Ibid.

9. Adam Shell, "Funds & Personal Finance," *Investor's Business Daily*, November 26, 1999.

10. Timothy Middleton, "Don't Let the 'Value' Label Fool You," *MSN Money*, February 2, 1999.

11. Richard C. Ten Wolde, "Most Valuable Player," *Barron's Online*, January 11, 1999.

12. Adam Shell, "Funds & Personal Finance," *Investor's Business Daily*, November 26, 1999.

13. Ibid.

14. *Outstanding Investor Digest*, December 31, 1999.

15. Adam Shell, "Funds & Personal Finance," *Investor's Business Daily*, November 26, 1999.

16. Kirk Kazanjian, *Wizards of Wall Street* (New York: New York Institute of Finance, 2000).

17. Ibid.

18. Mark Niemann, interview with author by telephone, December 13, 2001.

19. Sandra Ward, "Underpriced Market," *Barron's Online*, April 9, 2001.

20. Ibid.

21. "Value Preachers Spread the Gospel," *Fundsnet Insight*, Volume 8, Number 5, May 2001, p. 10.

22. Louis Rukeyser, "Bruised But Unbowed," *Louis Rukeyser's Mutual Funds*, January 2001.

CONCLUSION

1. William H. Miller III, *Legg Mason Value Trust Annual Report*, April 20, 1998.

2. Karen Damato and Aaron Lucchetti, "Bull Run: Mr. Miller of Legg Mason Will Beat S&P 500 for 9th Year in a Row," *Wall Street Journal*, December 31, 1999.

3. William H. Miller III, *Legg Mason Trust Annual Report*, March 31, 1995.

4. Adam Shell, "Funds & Personal Finance," *Investor's Business Daily*, November 26, 1999.

5. William H. Miller III, *Legg Mason Value Trust Inc., Special Investment Trust Inc., and Total Return Trust Inc. Annual Report*, March 31, 2000.

6. Benjamin Graham, *The Intelligent Investor*.

7. William H. Miller III, *Legg Mason Value Trust Annual Report*, March 31, 1991.

8. William H. Miller III, *Legg Mason Value Trust Annual Report*, April 14, 2000.

9. Joel Kurtzman, "An Interview with W. Brian Arthur," http://www.strategy-business.com/thoughtleaders/98209/page1.html.

10. Bill Miller, correspondence with author, December 5, 2001.

11. Louis Rukeyser, "Bruised But Unbowed," *Louis Rukeyser's Mutual Funds*, January 2001.

12. "To Beat the Market: Hire a Philosopher," *New York Times*, September 3, 1999.

GLOSSARY

Accounts Payable. Amounts owed on an open account for goods and/or services. Analysts examine the relationship of accounts payable to purchases as an indication of sound financial management.

Accounts Receivable. Money owed to a business for merchandise or services. This is a key factor in analyzing a company's liquidity, or its ability to meet current obligations without extra revenues.

Amortization. Accounting procedure that incrementally reduces the cost value of a limited life or intangible asset through periodic changes to income. This is the same as depreciation for fixed assets. For wasting assets, such as mineral deposits, this is called depletion.

Asset Play. A stock that is an attractive buy because the current price does not reflect the value of the company's assets. An example might be a motel chain in which the total value of the real estate is greater than the total market valuation. Such stocks often become takeover targets because they represent an easy way to acquire assets.

Balance Sheet. Financial report also known as "statement of condition" or "financial position." It is a snapshot of a company's assets, liabilities, and owners' equity on a specific date. Along with a profit and loss statement, a company is required to publish a balance sheet in its annual report for the benefit of shareholders.

Beta. A coefficient showing a company's relative volatility. It is a covariance of a stock in relation to the rest of the stock market.

Blend Funds. Managers of these funds look for stocks of growing companies selling at discount prices. They mix value and growth principles and are sometimes called core funds.

Book Value. (1) The value at which an asset is carried on the balance sheet. (2) The net asset value of a company's securities.

Capital Expenditures. Costs associated with maintaining the ongoing operations of the business. These usually include plant and equipment upgrades as old assets depreciate and become obsolete.

Cash Flow. The measure of the movement of money through a business. This number usually is reported at the end of a company's financial statement. A positive number means the company has generated cash rather than consumed it. A company with free cash flow has funds available for expansion, acquisitions, dividend payments, and so forth. A company with negative cash flow has to borrow money (at a cost) in order to expand the business. By the way, profitability doesn't ensure positive cash flow.

Convertibles. Corporate shares, usually preferred shares or bonds, which can be exchanged for a set number of some other security (usually common shares) at a set price. Sophisticated investors sometimes negotiate capital investments using convertibles to maximize income and minimize risk.

Core Funds. See **Blend funds**.

Cost of Capital. Rate of return a business could earn if it chose another investment with equivalent risk. Also called opportunity cost.

Debt Security. Security based on borrowed money that must be paid back, such as a bond or a debenture.

Debt-to-Equity Ratio. (1) Total liabilities divided by total shareholders' equity. This is an indication of how well equity can cushion creditors' claims in the event of liquidation. (2) Total long-term debt divided by total shareholders' equity. This is a measure of leverage, or how much borrowed money is being used to enhance invested capital. (3) Long-term debt and preferred stock divided by common stock equity. This gives a relationship between securities with a fixed payout and those with an unpredictable return.

Depreciation. Amortization of fixed assets, such as plant and equipment, to allocate the cost over the life of the asset. Depreciation reduces taxable income but does not reduce cash.

Discounted Cash Flow (DCF). The future value of expected cash receipts. The funds are discounted to reflect inflation, lost interest, and so on.

Dividend-Discount Model. A procedure for valuing the price of a stock by using predicted dividends and discounting them back to present value. The idea is that if the value obtained from the DDM is higher than the value at which the shares are currently trading, then the stock is undervalued.

EBITDA. Earnings before interest, taxes, depreciation, and amortization.

Efficient Market Theory. The notion that in today's information environment a stock's price reflects all knowledge about the security.

Extraordinary Item. Nonrecurring item that must be explained to investors, such as write-off of a closed division or bad investment, restructuring costs, or fraud. Earnings are usually reported both before and after the extraordinary item.

Free Cash Flow. Discretionary cash available to management. To figure it, start with net income from operations after tax, add depreciation and amortization, add or subtract as the case may be, changes in working capital, then subtract expenditures.

GAARP. Growth at a reasonable price. This is a conservative investment philosophy.

Generally Accepted Accounting Principles (GAAP). A set of accounting rules negotiated and agreed upon by regulators, companies, and accountants over a long period of time. GAAP is an attempt to set an accounting industry standard of fair and accurate financial reporting, and is the standard required by the Securities and Exchange Commission. For an alternative way of accounting, see **Pro-Forma Financial Reporting**.

Growth Funds. The fund managers seek stocks of companies whose earnings should grow faster than average. They assume stock prices will follow earnings. They pay little attention to standard measures of value as long as earnings increase rapidly.

Increasing Returns. The notion that the value of a product increases along with the number of people who are using it. The telephone is a good example of such a product. Used interchangeably with "network externalities."

Intrinsic Value. A security's true value based on the company's performance, regardless of the stock price. The valuation is determined by applying data to a valuation theory or model.

Lock-in. In technology, this refers to when consumers invest in a new technology or find some key element in a technology that requires them to use it for some time. They are therefore locked into the technology and the various products that are compatible with or enhance that technology.

Margin of Profit. Relationship of gross profits to net sales. Returns and allowances are subtracted from net sales. Cost of goods sold is subtracted from net sales to arrive at gross profit. Gross profit is then divided by net sales to get the profit margin. This is seen as a measure of efficiency and potential company profitability.

Market Capitalization. The value of a corporation based on the market price of its outstanding common stock, calculated by multiplying the number of outstanding shares by the current share price.

Modern Portfolio Theory. A sophisticated approach to investing that allows the investor to establish a relationship to and control risk and return. There is a built-in assumption that the higher the risk, the higher the reward. Attention is shifted from analysis of individual stocks to the statistical relationships between various stocks in a portfolio. Constant adjustments are made to securities holdings to minimize risk and maximize return.

Price-to-Book Ratio. The ratio of a stock's price to its book value per share. This ratio is obtained by dividing a stock's price per share by its book value (or net worth on the balance sheet). It is used as an indicator of whether a stock is over- or undervalued. Three or more is considered a high price-to-book ratio, but a company with that ratio may be a growth stock with limited assets and therefore minimal book value.

Price-to-Earnings Ratio. This is the price of a stock divided by its earnings per share. The P/E ratio is also called the "multiple," and it gives analysts an idea of how much is being paid for a company's earning power, or for a dollar's worth of its profits. Multiples of 20 or more are considered high.

Profit and Loss Statement. Shows a company's operating results over a period of time.

Pro-Forma Financial Reporting. Traditionally, a way of presenting earnings that would accurately describe a completely new business. These days, pro forma is a second set of accounting figures, conjured up outside GAAP, which presents a snapshot of the way a company would prefer to be perceived.

Relative Strength. A rating system that gives a numerical grade to every stock listed on the three major exchanges (New York Stock Exchange, American Stock Exchange, and Nasdaq) showing how that stock has performed in the previous 12 months in relation to all other stocks. The range is 1 to 99, with a high relative strength indicating a strong performance. A relative strength of 95, for example, indicates the stock has outperformed

95 percent of other U.S.-listed stocks in the past year. Relative strength reflects price momentum. *Investor's Business Daily* prints the relative strength for every stock every weekday.

Return on Equity. The return on invested capital, calculated by dividing a company's common stock equity into net income. Return on equity tells investors how efficiently their money is deployed.

Return on Invested Capital. The amount of money earned on a company's total capital expressed as a percentage. Return on invested capital often is used to compare companies in terms of efficient management and profitable goods and services.

Standard & Poor's Depository Receipt (Spider). The SPDE is similar to a closed-end index fund in which the holdings reflect the S&P 500 index. The Spider is an exchange-traded index that trades under the symbol SPY. For more information, refer to the web site www.nasdaq.com.

Standard & Poor's 500. The S&P 500 is an unmanaged index of common stock prices that includes reinvestment of dividends and capital gain distributions and is generally considered representative of the U.S. stock market. It is the index against which mutual funds are compared for performance evaluations.

Swarm Intelligence. Swarm intelligence (SI) is a characteristic of a system whereby collective behavior of the group, interacting with its environment, leads to coherent behavior. An example of swarm intelligence could be ants foraging for food and finding the quickest route from their nest to a food source. Another might be the system termites use to build a nest. There is evidence that the human immune system, interacting with the neurological system, operates on a theory of swarm intelligence. The stock market is considered another possible example of swarm behavior in human systems.

Total Return. The measurement of overall change in the value of an investment including changes in share price and dividends. For a mutual fund, the definition is the same, except it also includes any capital gains distributions and assumes reinvestment of dividends. **Average Annual Total Return** is the average annual compounded return that would have produced the same cumulative total return if the fund's performance had been constant over the entire period. **Cumulative Total Return** shows total return over a specific period of time.

Valuation. Placing a value, worth, or price on an asset, such as a common stock.

Value Fund. A value manager ferrets out stock whose price is low in relation to its earnings. Typically these companies have had lagging earnings or are in some other kind of trouble. The investor feels the stock price has been beat down more than it deserves and that a recovery is at hand.

Value of an Investment. The present value of the future free cash flow of that investment.

Versioning. A strategy that enables a company to distinguish its products from the competition and protect its prices from collapse. Usually this involves tailoring different versions of the same core of information for different end users.

Working Capital. A company's cash, accounts receivable, inventory, and other current assets. Working capital finances the cash conversion cycle of a business—the time needed to convert raw materials into finished goods, sales, accounts receivable, and finally, cash. Companies with plentiful working capital can survive the vicissitudes of unpredictable business cycles.

SUGGESTED READING

Thomas Bass, *The Eudaemonic Pie*, iuniverse, 2000.

John Henry Clippinger, *The Biology of Business: Decoding the Natural Laws of Enterprise*, Jossey-Bass Inc., 1999.

Earnshaw Cook, *Percentage Baseball*, Cambridge, MA: MIT Press, 1966.

Benjamin Graham, *The Intelligent Investor*, New York: McGraw-Hill, 1949.

Benjamin Graham and David L. Dodd, *Security Analysis: The Classic 1934 Edition*, New York: McGraw-Hill.

Gary Gray, Patrick J. Cusatis, and J. Randall Woolridge, *Streetsmart Guide to Valuing a Stock*, New York: McGraw-Hill, 1999.

Robert G. Hagstrom, *Latticework: The New Investing*, Texere, 2000.

James Kennedy, et al, *Swarm Intelligence*, Morgan Kaufmann Publishers, 2001.

Ray Kurzweil, *The Age of Spiritual Machines*, New York: Viking Penguin, 1999.

Janet Lowe, *Benjamin Graham on Value Investing: Lessons from the Dean of Wall Street*, New York: Penguin Books, 1994.

Louis Menand, *The Metaphysical Club: A Story of Ideas in America*, Farrar, Straus & Giroux, 2001.

Adam Smith, *The Money Game*, New York: Random House, 1976.

Edward Allen Toppel, *Zen in the Markets*, New York: Warner Books, 1994.

Timothy P. Vick, *Wall Street on Sale: How to Beat the Market as a Value Investor*, New York: McGraw-Hill, March, 2001.

John Burr Williams, *The Theory of Investment Value*, 1938. Reprinted by Fraser Publishing Co., 1997.

Erwin Schrödinger, *Nature and the Greeks*, Cambridge University Press, 1954.

Hal R. Varian and Carl Shapiro, *Information Rules: A Strategic Guide to the Network Economy*, Cambridge, MA: Harvard Business School Press, 1998.

INDEX

255

Index

Index